ATHENS CITY SCHOOLS

SCHOOL_____ DATE OF PURCHASE 9/82 COST 8.99

SUBJECT_____ GRADE_____ BOOK NO. 82-74

COMPANY PURCHASED FROM Baker & Taylor

MORRISON ELEMENTARY SCHOOL
ROUTE 1, BOX 47
ATHENS, OHIO 45701-9708

BODYWORKS

The Kids' Guide to Food and Physical Fitness

BODYWORKS

The Kids' Guide to Food and Physical Fitness

by Carol Bershad and Deborah Bernick
with illustrations by Heidi Johanna Selig

Random House 🏠 **New York**

A Note to Teachers

Bodyworks was written as part of an upper elementary curriculum package which is available for purchase. The package includes this book under its original title, *From the Inside Out*, as well as a Teachers' Guide and Resource Manual, worksheet masters, illustrated vocabulary cards, and posters.

For further information, please contact:

Learning for Life/MSH
Department BW
141 Tremont Street
Boston, Massachusetts 02111

Bodyworks was produced in the public schools of Newton, Massachusetts, as part of the Learning for Life Project. Its development was funded by the Massachusetts Department of Education, under ESEA Title IV C, and by the W. K. Kellogg Foundation, under a grant for Management Sciences for Health.

Ann Buxbaum, *Editor and Learning for Life Project Director*
Nuria Morey, *Editorial Assistant*
Pat Granahan, *Nutrition Consultant*
Caroline Saltonstall, *Art Director*
Diane C. Fiedler, *Production Assistant*
Paul M. Levy, *Letterer*
Allan O' Brien Denchfield, *Animator*

Rachel Feilden, *Project Evaluator*
Nirmala Murthy, *Project Evaluator*
Ronald O'Connor, M.D., *Kellogg Project Director*

Library of Congress Cataloging in Publication Data:
Bershad, Carol. Bodyworks: the kids' guide to food and physical fitness. First published in 1979 under title: From the inside out. SUMMARY: Covers lifestyles, how the body works, physical fitness, sources of food, eating habits, and nutrition. 1. Health—Juvenile literature. 2. Body, Human—Juvenile literature. 3. Nutrition—Juvenile literature. 4. Physical fitness—Juvenile literature. [1. Health. 2. Body, Human. 3. Nutrition. 4. Physical fitness] I. Bernick, Deborah, joint author. II. Selig, Heidi Johanna. III. Title. RA777.B47 1981 613.2 80-26741
ISBN: 0-394-84752-0 (trade); 0-394-94752-5 (lib. bdg.)
Manufactured in the United States of America 1 2 3 4 5 6 7 8 9 0

Table of Contents

You are many things — a muscle mover,
root picker,
blood pumper,
food-talker,
calorie burner,
and
protein maker.

You are pretty amazing. You're all these things, and more. You're a walking, talking, munching, crunching story — a story that changes every minute of the day.

This book will help you listen to the story your body can tell you inside and out. The book also has a few fantastic food and fitness tales of its own. Read about:

- The Trapper with the "See-Through" Stomach
- The Rabbi Who Set a World Rope-Jumping Record
- Liver Lovers Who Lost Layers
- The Four-Legged Milk Machine from Roaring Springs, and
- How to Become a Cat, a Cobra, or a Swan.

This is not a book with all the answers. It's a Stop, Listen, and Do book. Explore your own food and physical fitness lifestyle. Learn the value of different foods and fitness activities. **Choose a lifestyle that can keep you healthy and fit for a lifetime.** Find your own answers and then write your own story.

You'll meet a lot of interesting characters along the way, but the most important one is you! What kind of food and fitness tale will you tell?

LIFESTYLES

1

An Early American Day

Take a look at a day in the lives of two imaginary kids from Massachusetts, Laura and Jimmy, who lived about 150 years apart. As you read, try to get a picture of how they worked, traveled, and played. Think about how they prepared their food and what they ate. Did they use their own energy or energy from machines?

Afterward, take a closer look at how you spend *your* time. Fill out "The Time of Your Life" worksheet for a day in your life. Compare your physical activities and the time you spend preparing and eating food with what you found out about Laura and Jimmy.

* * *

It is a crisp Thursday morning in October, 1820, in a small Massachusetts town. Laura has a busy day ahead helping with family chores and getting ready for her birthday celebration tomorrow.

Laura awakens at sunrise and tumbles down from her loft to begin her morning work. She fetches a pail of water from the pump in the yard and gathers fresh eggs from the henhouse. Laura and her younger brother take turns milking the cow and carrying in logs for the fireplace. They will not be going to school today because the whole family is needed to help with the chores and harvesting.

Laura and her four brothers sit down to a heavy breakfast of leftover stew, corncakes, and apple cider. When they finish eating, her brothers head out to chop some firewood. They will also help their father bring the animals out to pasture and mend the fences. In the meantime, Laura washes the dishes and sweeps the house, and then goes to work with her mother in the kitchen garden.

Laura picks ripe pumpkins and squash off the vines near the house and pulls up carrots and turnips nearby. Then she carries several loads of these vegetables down to the root cellar to store away for the long winter months ahead. She and her mother will be drying corn and beans out in the sun later this week, and stringing up apples to dry in the attic over Laura's bed.

By mid-morning, it is time to churn the butter for the apple pies for her party. Laura skims the cream off a jug of fresh milk and pours it into a large wooden churn. She sings out, "Come, butter, come," as she pushes the heavy dasher up and down for half an hour, working hard until the creamy butter finally appears. Laura and her mother mix the butter with flour and water to make enough pie dough for several pies. They roll out the dough, fill it with apples from the orchard, and put the pies in the oven to bake golden brown.

Around one o'clock, Laura helps her mother serve the family the midday meal. Her father and brothers come back from their work in the fields to share a dinner of salt beef, squash, carrots, and corn bread. The dessert is a special treat of Indian pudding made with eggs, cornmeal, and a bit of the molasses that Laura's mother traded several wheels of cheese to buy. Lunch is the main meal of the day, a time when the whole family can get together to talk and rest before the afternoon work begins. Supper will be a light meal, with meat and vegetables depending on the season.

During the afternoon, Laura walks a mile down the road to invite her neighbor's family to the party. They promise to come after they finish helping out at a barn-raising. On her way back, Laura passes some farmers in their wagons riding to the market in town. A group of children are playing tag and rolling hoops nearby. Laura has no time to join them today, since she has to finish all her chores before sundown.

By the end of the day, the whole family is tired. On a long summer evening, there might still be enough daylight for Laura to work on her corn husk doll or for her brothers to whittle away at their walking sticks and whistles. But darkness comes early in the fall, and candles are too expensive to use for unnecessary activities. Besides, everyone needs to get a good night's rest tonight before the big party tomorrow. By eight o'clock, the whole family is sound asleep.

The Day Before Jimmy's Birthday

Come spend an autumn Thursday in the 1980's with Jimmy, who is turning 11 tomorrow. He has a million things to do before his birthday party this weekend.

His alarm clock goes off at 7:15. During the next half hour, Jimmy washes and gets dressed. Then he heads downstairs for breakfast. First he opens a can of frozen orange juice and adds water from the tap. Then Jimmy pours out a bowl of his favorite cereal and slices some fruit on top. It takes him only fifteen minutes to gulp down his breakfast and brush his teeth with his electric tooth brush.

Since his parents are busy getting ready for work, Jimmy packs his own lunch — a peanut butter and jelly sandwich, a package of potato chips, and a piece of fruit. Then he runs outside to catch up with his friends on their way to school.

Classes begin at 8:30. Schoolwork keeps Jimmy busy at his desk during most of the day. The only active break he gets is fifteen minutes during recess when he plays touch football. On the way back into the building after recess, Jimmy talks to his friends about the new bike he just got as a birthday present from his parents. Now he and his sister can bike over to the Saturday soccer games together.

At three o'clock, Jimmy's mom picks him up at school. They drive to the new shopping mall, where they spend a couple of hours buying favors for his party and deciding how Jimmy will use the birthday money his grandparents sent him. After looking over the hundreds of toys in the store, Jimmy finally chooses a new electronic game he saw advertised on TV.

On the way back home they meet his dad for a quick hamburger, fries, and a milkshake at a fast-food restaurant. Then they stop at the supermarket to pick up a box of cake mix and a half-dozen eggs for the chocolate cake Jimmy and his mom will bake tonight. Because of all the rush-hour traffic on the roads, it takes them almost 45 minutes to drive home.

As soon as they get in the door, Jimmy calls up a friend to talk about the party. If it is sunny on Saturday, they will go on a picnic. If it rains, they will cram into his dad's station wagon and drive over to see the latest movie that everyone is talking about.

When he gets off the phone a half-hour later, Jimmy heads upstairs to do his homework and vacuum his room — finally! In the meantime, his dad and mom empty the dishwasher. At 8:30, Jimmy's mom calls upstairs, "Baking time!" and Jimmy bounds down the stairs. He rips open the cake mix box, adds water and eggs, and watches his mother beat the cake batter with the electric mixer. He uses the electric can opener to open a can of chocolate frosting, and he uses his fingers to sneak in a few sweet licks now and then.

By 9:30 p.m., Jimmy is ready to call it a day. He has a half hour to kill before bedtime. There are no worthwhile programs on TV tonight, so he reads for a while and plays with his new game before he drops off to sleep. Everything is set for the big day.

The Time of Your Life

Keep a Time Chart to get a clearer picture of your own daily lifestyle.

Pick a weekday this week to record all your daily activities, from the time you get up until you fall asleep. From 6 a.m. on, write down each activity and the time you spend doing it (in minutes). Make a chart like the one below.

At the top of your sheet, write down the number of hours you slept the night before.

At the bottom of each side of your paper, add up a subtotal in minutes for each category. Divide by 60 to get the subtotals in hours. Add your two subtotals together to get a **final total** in hours for each category.

Jimmy's Day

Time of Day	Activity	Sleeping	Eating	Schoolwork	Chores (washing, dressing, housework, yard work, shopping)	Active (playing, biking, walking, running, dancing)	Quiet (reading, riding in a car or bus, playing quiet games, relaxing)	TV
the night before	sleeping	8 hrs.						
6 a.m.	sleeping	60 min.						
7 a.m.	sleeping washed and dressed ate breakfast	15 min.	15 min.		30 min.			
8 a.m.	walked to school played in playground schoolwork			30 min.		15 min. 15 min.		
9 a.m. to 3 p.m.	schoolwork — estimates lunch		15 min	5 hrs. 15 min.				

Make a pie chart with 24 sections, like the one below.

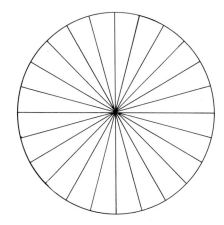

Make a color or pattern key for each category of activity.

 Sleeping

 Schoolwork

 Active Time

 TV

 Eating

 Chores

 Quiet Time

MY CAT CRAZY'S LIFESTYLE

Now color in the amount of time you spent on each category.

MY DAY

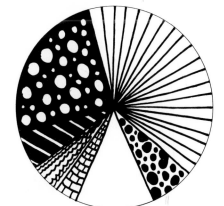

Pattern Key:

Chasing her tail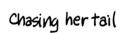

Eating

Sleeping

MAKE A LIST

of all the machines you used yesterday. How many helped you do <u>work</u>? How many were for <u>transportation</u>? Did any affect how you <u>play</u>?

alarm clock
remote control TV
electric can opener
refrigerator
power lawn mower
dishwasher
vacuum cleaner
computerized closet cleaner
Harry the homework robot

MACHINES MINUS TWO

Try to live without using two of the regular machines in your life for one week. Find ways to use your own human energy instead. Are you getting more exercise than you usually do? Ask your parents and friends to try this and see how they do.

Stop and think how Laura or Jimmy would complete a Time Chart for *their* daily schedules. Would their physical activities be mainly chores or recreation? Take a look at how Laura and Jimmy's mealtimes compare with yours. How much of their time would be spent preparing food? Make a list of all the foods Laura's family grew or produced on their land. Were these available in every season? How do Jimmy's food choices compare to Laura's?

If you could ask Laura to tell you about her "homework," she would probably talk about churning butter or weeding the garden. How do you think she would feel about the way your family washes clothes, stores away food, or keeps the lawn trimmed? Laura didn't always have time for schoolwork and play activities. Does Jimmy? Do you?

Some surveys show that Americans have an average of five hours of free time each day, with slightly more free time for kids than adults. The Time Chart averages for the kids in one fifth-grade class looked like this:

SLEEPING: 10 hours	CHORES: 1 hour
EATING: 1½ hours	ACTIVE TIME: 1¼ hours
SCHOOLWORK: 5¾ hours	QUIET TIME: 3½ hours
	TV: 1 hour

How does that compare with Jimmy's day and *your* day?

You may get a few clues about the difference between Laura's and Jimmy's days by thinking about the way machines affect our lifestyles today. **In the past 100 years, machines in American factories and labor-saving devices in homes have taken over much of the physical work that people used to do themselves.** Over the past fifteen years, the average American family spends 1/5 less time doing housework than it used to. Do you buy ready-made shirts and socks at a department store or processed foods like bread and frozen vegetables at the supermarket? Most of these items were made or assembled by machines before they reached your home. Your body only has to wear — or eat — what you bought.

Machines like cars and buses have also replaced foot power. How often do you use the muscle power of your arms, legs, and feet? Laura and her brothers must have given these

muscles a good workout when they walked places, worked outdoors, or ran after a stray cow. Think about how Jimmy does errands for his party. Do you often go to stores by car and use escalators or elevators once you are inside? Do you ever use your bike to get places, or would you rather ride in a car or bus?

Inventions on the Move

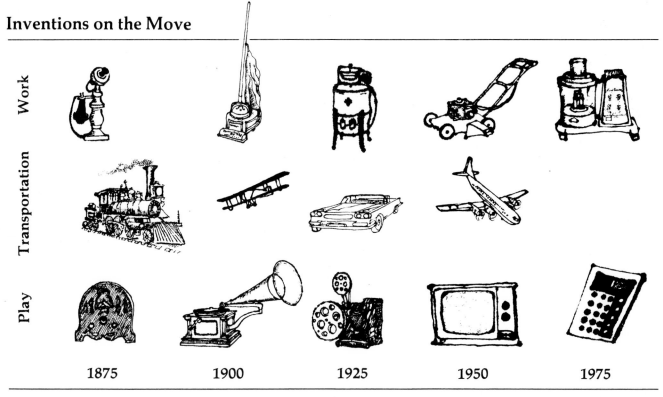

| | 1875 | 1900 | 1925 | 1950 | 1975 |

Since your body is a special kind of machine built for action, it needs exercise and movement in order to work right. If your muscles don't get enough practice lifting, carrying, moving, throwing, or pulling, they get weaker and do less for you when you need an extra jump in a volleyball game or a boost in carrying a bag of groceries.

An active lifestyle helps keep you in shape. It makes it easier for you to move hard and fast when you need to. Think about that the next time you're running after a school bus or chasing a speeding frisbee.

Fit Tips

Since your parents may not have asked you to carry firewood lately and your drinking water comes straight from the

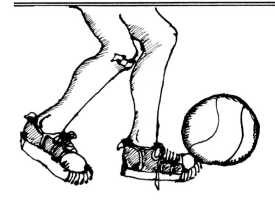

tap, how can you make sure to put enough exercise into your day to stay in shape?

One way is to **build extra activity into your free time.** Think about how you spend your weekends. Would you rather watch a sport or play it? Sports stadiums in the U.S. fill up over 100 million seats each year with sedentary super-sitters. Some big sports events on TV like the Super Bowl or the World Series attract over 65 million viewers at one sitting — one out of every three Americans. Instead of just exercising your eyeballs watching the pros play, give your *own* body a work-out for a change.

When you're ready for action, **choose games that really keep you moving,** and not watching from the sidelines. Are there new games you can bring home from gym and get going with friends in your neighborhood? The sports activities and personal fitness boosts described in the next chapter may give you some ideas.

Take a look at your Time Chart. Are there places in the Chores and Quiet Time categories where you can fit in some extra activity you didn't have before? **How much TV-watching shows up in your schedule?** The average kid your age may spend two to three hours a day watching TV, over 1/3 of his or her free time. **Are there any active substitutes for a change of pace?** One man hooked up his TV to an exercise bicycle so that he could only watch when he made enough electricity by pedalling the bike!

How about blazing new trails in your life? That means **walking** whenever you get the chance. **Get out of the car early** on your way to a movie or a friend's house. Ask your parents to **park far away** when you go shopping, and **use the stairs** once you get inside the store. Explore your neighborhood with your friends, or find a nearby trail where you can **see nature on foot.** Do you like to hike or bike? Are there cross-country ski trails in the woods near where you live? Some of those trails will take you through beautiful countryside to places that you could never explore in a car.

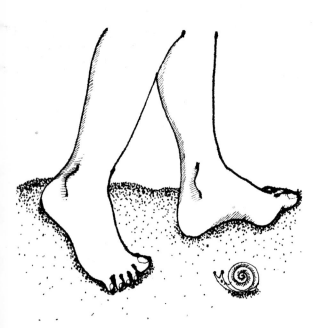

Here are a few examples of what people in other places are doing. In Japan, schools have two exercise breaks each day so

students can get up and stretch between lessons. In China, nearly everyone, including grandparents and small children, exercises in the parks and on the sidewalks of the cities. In Sweden, many women who work at home attend exercise programs in the afternoons in their nearby supermarkets.

In Laura's day, most Americans were farmers who worked to grow their own food. Today, over half the working people in this country have sit-down jobs, with little chance to move around. **What are people your parents' age doing to build an active lifestyle?** In Sweden, many offices and factories have gyms where people can take an active lunch break learning gymnastics, swimming, or playing ball. Some offices even have walking and running contests organized by the employees. A few American companies are starting to build gyms and set up exercise programs in their buildings, too.

Think about how many different ways you can make *your* lifestyle an active one. You have many more choices about how to spend your free time than kids did a few hundred years ago. So, next time you are wondering what to do, **make a choice that really keeps your body on the move!**

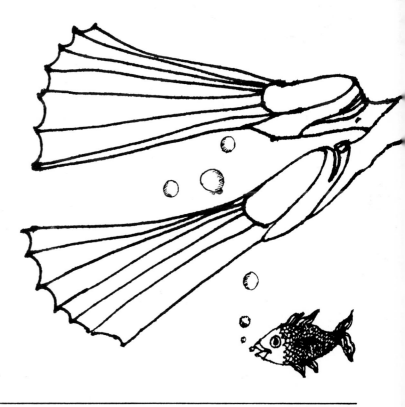

YOUR BODY ON THE MOVE

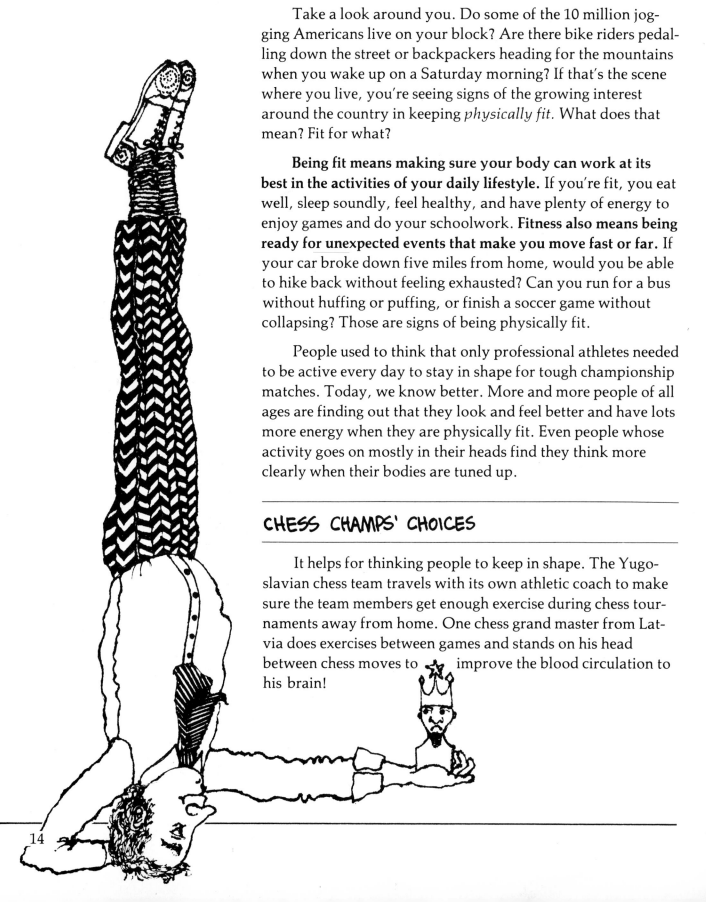

Take a look around you. Do some of the 10 million jogging Americans live on your block? Are there bike riders pedalling down the street or backpackers heading for the mountains when you wake up on a Saturday morning? If that's the scene where you live, you're seeing signs of the growing interest around the country in keeping *physically fit.* What does that mean? Fit for what?

Being fit means making sure your body can work at its best in the activities of your daily lifestyle. If you're fit, you eat well, sleep soundly, feel healthy, and have plenty of energy to enjoy games and do your schoolwork. **Fitness also means being ready for unexpected events that make you move fast or far.** If your car broke down five miles from home, would you be able to hike back without feeling exhausted? Can you run for a bus without huffing or puffing, or finish a soccer game without collapsing? Those are signs of being physically fit.

People used to think that only professional athletes needed to be active every day to stay in shape for tough championship matches. Today, we know better. More and more people of all ages are finding out that they look and feel better and have lots more energy when they are physically fit. Even people whose activity goes on mostly in their heads find they think more clearly when their bodies are tuned up.

CHESS CHAMPS' CHOICES

It helps for thinking people to keep in shape. The Yugoslavian chess team travels with its own athletic coach to make sure the team members get enough exercise during chess tournaments away from home. One chess grand master from Latvia does exercises between games and stands on his head between chess moves to improve the blood circulation to his brain!

Before the world chess championships in 1972, Bobby Fischer and Boris Spassky spent months in physical training. Fischer spent part of each day swimming, playing tennis, skipping rope, lifting weights, riding an exercycle, and pounding on a 300-pound bag. Spassky chose to run, swim, and do yoga stretching exercises. ⸺

You may not notice any 50-year-old Major League baseball stars, but you can find many energetic grandmas and grandpas riding bikes, hiking in the woods, climbing mountains, and even running. They are having fun and building up their level of fitness at the same time. These are activities that people can begin to do as children and enjoy throughout their lives.

A GRANDMA IN GREAT SHAPE

Grandma Emma Gatewood was a 67-year-old mother of eleven when she first decided to walk the entire length of the Appalachian Trail in 1955. She hiked 2,000 miles over the mountains and through the woods from Georgia to Maine in 145 days. Along the way, she lost 30 pounds and wore out five pairs of sneakers.

How did Grandma Gatewood get in shape for the big event? She insisted that it took no special training. It's likely that her years growing up on a farm and then leading an active lifestyle made it possible for her to be physically fit even into her 60's.

She went back and walked the Trail at the age of 70, to become the first woman to do it twice. Then, to celebrate her 71st birthday and the 100th anniversary of the Oregon Trail, she walked the entire 2,000 miles of that trail, too. ⸺

What exactly does fitness mean about the way your body works? Take a trip inside your heart, your other muscles, and your lungs. Learn more about the body signs that tell you what each activity is doing *for* you. When you get to know your insides better, you'll have a running start on fitness for life.

LEARNING FOR LIFE

Interview two people your grandparents' age who keep in shape. What do they do to keep fit? When did they start? Why do they keep it up?

What Shape Are You In?

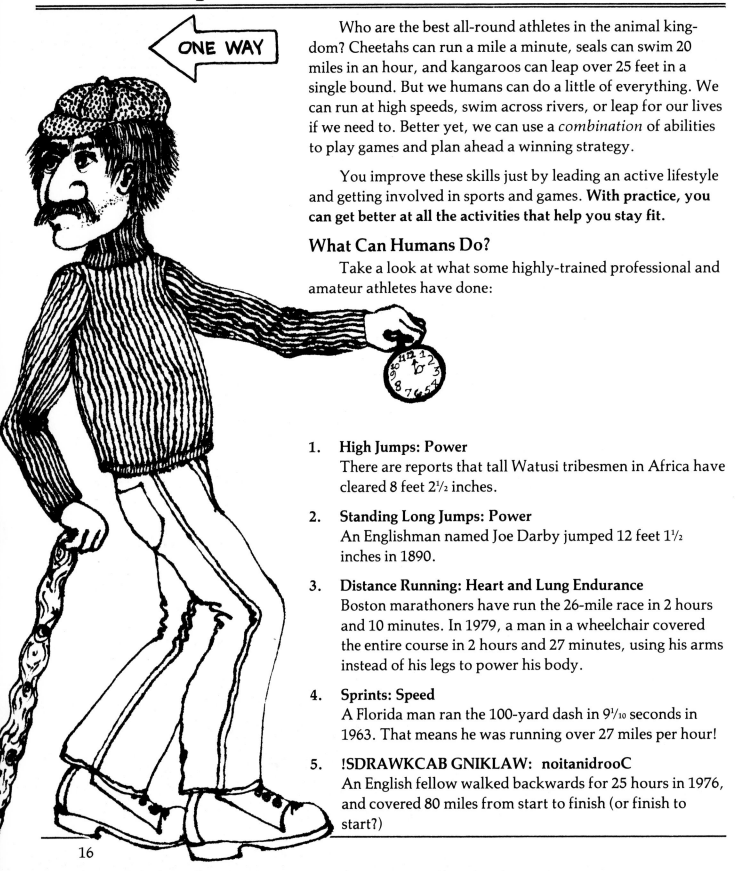

ONE WAY

Who are the best all-round athletes in the animal kingdom? Cheetahs can run a mile a minute, seals can swim 20 miles in an hour, and kangaroos can leap over 25 feet in a single bound. But we humans can do a little of everything. We can run at high speeds, swim across rivers, or leap for our lives if we need to. Better yet, we can use a *combination* of abilities to play games and plan ahead a winning strategy.

You improve these skills just by leading an active lifestyle and getting involved in sports and games. **With practice, you can get better at all the activities that help you stay fit.**

What Can Humans Do?

Take a look at what some highly-trained professional and amateur athletes have done:

1. **High Jumps: Power**
   There are reports that tall Watusi tribesmen in Africa have cleared 8 feet 2½ inches.

2. **Standing Long Jumps: Power**
   An Englishman named Joe Darby jumped 12 feet 1½ inches in 1890.

3. **Distance Running: Heart and Lung Endurance**
   Boston marathoners have run the 26-mile race in 2 hours and 10 minutes. In 1979, a man in a wheelchair covered the entire course in 2 hours and 27 minutes, using his arms instead of his legs to power his body.

4. **Sprints: Speed**
   A Florida man ran the 100-yard dash in 9¹/₁₀ seconds in 1963. That means he was running over 27 miles per hour!

5. **!SDRAWKCAB GNIKLAW: noitanidrooC**
   An English fellow walked backwards for 25 hours in 1976, and covered 80 miles from start to finish (or finish to start?)

What can *your* body do when you really put it to work? Get a clearer picture of your body's talents in action. Try out the activities on the next two pages to see what you can do now. No matter what you find, with concentration and regular training you can improve your skills in all these areas in a few months' time.

Check yourself out in the **four main fitness areas: heart and lung endurance, muscle endurance, flexibility, and strength.** Also test your motor skills of agility, speed, and power. Keep track of how you do in each of these activities. In six or eight weeks, try them again to see whether they have become easier.

My Motion Picture

Bring a yardstick with you when you try these first two. A friend can also help on the Heads Up/Legs Up, Bent Leg Sit-Ups, Wall Jump, and Down the Block.

Activity	Benefit	Skill	HOW DID I DO?			
			Date	First try	Date	Second try
1. See your knee	Flexibility	Inches to right knee	9/20	6 inches	11/4	4 inches
		Inches to left knee		5½ inches		4½ inches

1. **See Your Knee**
    (Flexibility — forward bending)
    Sit on the floor with your legs wide apart. Bend forward slowly and reach with both hands for one of your ankles. Keep your legs straight. Can your head reach your knee? How many inches away from your knee are you? Try it with your other leg.

HEADS UP/LEGS UP

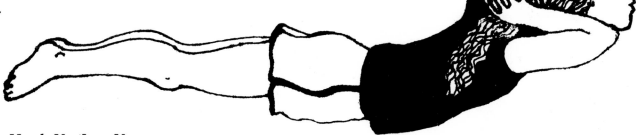

2. **Heads Up/Legs Up**
    (Flexibility — backward bending)
    Lie face down on a mat or folded blanket. With your

PUSH-UP

hands clasped behind your neck, slowly raise your chin and chest off the floor. How high can you go? Ask a friend with a yardstick to measure the distance from your chin to the floor.

Now lie down again, with your arms at your sides. Keep your legs straight, toes pointed. Raise your legs in the air. How high can your legs get off the ground? Ask your friend to measure the distance from the tip of your toes to the floor.

3. **Push-Ups**
(Arm strength and endurance)
Lie on your stomach, hands under your shoulders, feet on tip-toes. Raise your body off the ground, keeping your back straight. Come down to the starting position and repeat. How many push-ups can you do in 30 seconds?

4. **Standing Broad Jump**
(Leg power)
How are the springs in your legs? Do a standing broad jump to see. Find a grassy area and lay down a piece of string for a starting line. Leap forward as far as you can. Drop a coin to measure the distance from where your heel lands to the starting line. Did you travel farther than your height? A jump of over 5 feet is excellent for 10- to 12-year-olds.

5. **Bent Leg Sit-Ups**
(Abdominal strength and endurance)
Lie on your back with knees bent and hands clasped behind your head. Ask a friend to hold your feet down. Slowly raise your trunk and touch your elbows to your knees. Come down again and then repeat. How many bent leg sit-ups can you do?

BENT LEG SIT-UP

6. Wall Jump
(Leg power and arm flexibility)

Stand facing a wall. Place both hands over your head and stretch as high as you can on tiptoes. Ask a friend to mark the spot where you touch the wall. Face the wall again. Crouch down and then jump as high as you can. Have that friend mark this spot too. Measure the distance between the two marks.

7. Run and Weave
(Agility)

How quickly can your body change directions? Place 5 books about 5 feet apart in a straight line. On your mark, get set, go! Run around the books on your way forward and back. How many laps can you do in 1 minute without touching any books? Reverse directions. How many did you do this time?

8. Down the Block
(Speed)

Run a set distance like 100 yards as fast as you can. Have a friend keep track of your time. With a little running practice, can you beat your own record a few weeks later?

9. Jump Rope Marathon
(Heart and lung endurance; arm and leg endurance; coordination)

Take out a jump rope and a watch. Jump as long as you can before you get tired. Record the time on your worksheet. If you'd rather not jump over a rope, try jumping over a line on one side, then the other.

10. Nine Moving Minutes
(Heart and lung endurance)

How far can you jog-walk before you get tired? Do a few minutes of the runners' warm-ups on page 27. Pick a route you can measure like your school track or the way to and from your friend's house. Start jogging. Jog slowly enough so you can talk. When you feel tired, switch to a walk; then jog again as soon as you get back your energy. Measure how far you go in exactly nine minutes. If you can't tell the exact distance, remember a landmark (a tree, a house) that marks the spot where you stopped.

WALL JUMP

— You

Me —

You —

Muscles Making the Moves

KEEP SMILING

It takes 34 muscles to frown and only 13 to smile.

Whenever you jump for a basket or pedal a bike, muscles are moving the bones in your body to get you where you want to go. **You have a total of 600 muscles working together in different combinations.** There are over 100 of them in your face and neck alone, helping you smile, laugh, eat, look around, and cry. Wag your tongue and you are wiggling a bundle of muscles.

When you are out on the soccer field, how do your leg muscles know when to kick a ball and how far to send it? Your eyes follow the ball and send signals to the brain. The brain sends a chemical message along the nerveways to the particular *muscle fibers* that you want to move. These fibers are long, thin cells that lie alongside each other like spaghetti in a box. **Bundles of muscle fibers form the major muscle groups in your body** (including the leg muscles that you get such a kick out of using!).

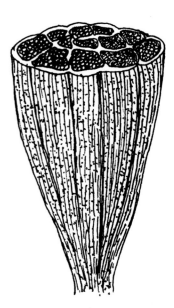

muscle fibers

bundle of muscle fibers

muscle group

When you're ready to move, brain messages signal certain muscle fibers to contract (shorten). They do that within a few hundredths of a second. In between contracting acts, they relax. **An individual muscle can do only these two things — contract and relax.** This means that a muscle can only pull, not push.

Muscles work in pairs. If you want to use a muscle as a pusher, your brain sends messages to its partner, another muscle that lies opposite it (often on the other side of a bone). That second muscle can then contract and move the body part in the opposite direction, while the first muscle relaxes.

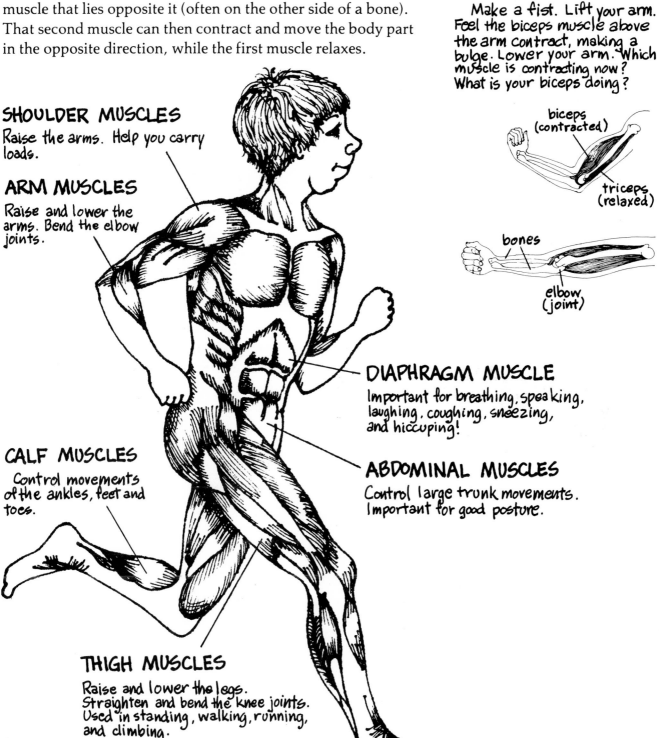

SHOULDER MUSCLES
Raise the arms. Help you carry loads.

ARM MUSCLES
Raise and lower the arms. Bend the elbow joints.

CALF MUSCLES
Control movements of the ankles, feet and toes.

THIGH MUSCLES
Raise and lower the legs. Straighten and bend the knee joints. Used in standing, walking, running, and climbing.

BEND YOUR ARM
Make a fist. Lift your arm. Feel the biceps muscle above the arm contract, making a bulge. Lower your arm. Which muscle is contracting now? What is your biceps doing?

biceps (contracted)

triceps (relaxed)

bones

elbow (joint)

DIAPHRAGM MUSCLE
Important for breathing, speaking, laughing, coughing, sneezing, and hiccuping!

ABDOMINAL MUSCLES
Control large trunk movements. Important for good posture.

Lifestyle Links

When you carry groceries or pedal hard on a bike, you are giving your muscles the kind of workout they were built for. **Muscles get smaller and weaker when you ignore them by letting them rest too much.** If you ever broke your leg or arm and couldn't wait to get the cast off, you were probably surprised to see how limp and weak your leg or arm muscles had become in a few weeks' time.

Usually your muscles are slightly contracted and ready for action. This gives them their firmness which we call *muscle tone.* When muscles relax completely inside a cast, they lose their muscle tone and become flabby. The stomach and buttocks are two areas where many people who don't exercise lose their muscle tone. If they start exercising these muscles, their bodies become firmer.

FAR-OUT FITNESS

What would happen if your lifestyle changed drastically and you were stuck in a small capsule for weeks on end? That's the story of the astronauts who went up in space in the first Skylab space flight in 1973. Since they couldn't move far, their muscles and their hearts got less exercise than usual. As a result, the astronauts felt weak and walked with a wobble when they first arrived back on earth.

Scientists learned from them how much the human body needs movement in order to stay healthy. During the next two Skylab trips, the astronauts did 90 minutes of bicycle-pedalling exercises every day. After 84 days in space, they arrived back almost as fit as when they began their trip.

THE FITNESS FOUR

Muscle strength
Muscle endurance
Flexibility
Heart and lung endurance
(cardio-respiratory endurance)

Muscle Strength — The One-Shot Deal

The Superman look-alike contest has hit your school and you've decided to put your muscles to an extraordinary test. During recess, you will bend a bar of Kryptonite in your bare hands. What gives you the super boost you need?

As you strain and push to bend the bar, you call on all the available muscle fibers in your hands that normally wait by the sidelines. You are using the full strength of your hand and arm muscles. **Strength is the maximum amount of work muscles can do in a single effort.**

If you can make a pretzel out of the Kryptonite bar in three seconds flat, you've got muscle power. **Power is the skill of using your muscle strength very quickly.** Your leg power helps you do a standing broad jump or a wall jump. You use arm power every time you send a baseball speeding over to a waiting first baseman.

Muscle Endurance — In the Long Run

Muscle endurance is how well a group of muscles can continue to work for a long period of time. Good arm muscle endurance helps you carry a heavy load of books all the way to school without getting tired. Good leg muscle endurance can get you through a long disco dance.

There are two ways to measure muscle endurance. The first is to see *how many times* you can repeat a movement in a number of seconds or minutes. The other way is to see *how long* you can stay in a certain position over time. You might be able to lift a half-ton elephant up on your feet. But could you keep him up there for half an hour while a fiddler played a folk dance? That's leg endurance!

People often focus on muscle strength and endurance when they set up a fitness program. Actually, experts tell us that strength and endurance are only *part* of the way you keep your body in shape. They only affect the exact muscles you use each time. If you work on the muscle strength of your arms, your legs don't get stronger from the exercise. Baseball players build up arm strength when they take practice swings on weighted bats, but they have to do bending and stretching movements to give their *whole body* a workout.

Hustle that Muscle

When you get out and play almost every day, you build up your muscle strength and endurance. As you begin doing new activities like dancing, gymnastics, rope-jumping or swimming, you start to use muscle fibers that used to be inactive. As you use them, these **muscle fibers get thicker** and are able to do extra work for you. They can even hold loads of up to 1,000 times their own weight if a real emergency occurs.

MUSCLE RIDDLE
Who has more arm muscles - a weight lifter or a ten-pound baby?
(See page 210 for the answer)

Will your muscles continue to gain in strength and endurance if you give them the same amount of exercise at sports and games every week? You'll get a little more practice at skills and gain some strength. But you'll soon reach your limit. **For muscles to keep getting stronger, you need to apply the overload principle.** This means that you gradually increase *how often, how hard,* or *how long* you use a particular muscle group.

Weightlifters do this when they start by lifting a 10-pound weight five times, then ten times. Then they switch to a 12-pound weight five times and increase the number of lifts again. Athletes apply the overload principle during their training periods. Each day they increase their workload by exercising longer and harder. This helps them get in shape at least one or two months before the competitive season begins.

Conditioning programs are reversible. A person in good shape can lose a lot of strength and endurance in just two or three weeks of inactivity. A soccer star who gets the flu will need extra training sessions to catch up with his former fitness level. Many ex-baseball and football players who don't exercise lose all the muscular benefits they had when they were

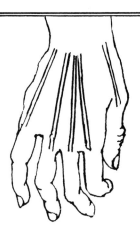

TOUCH A TENDON

Watch some tendons dance around on the back of your hand as you tap your fingers lightly on the table.

Feel your Achilles tendon tighten on the back of your ankle as you bend your knees. (Achilles was a Greek hero whose ankle tendon was the only weak part of him. He died when he was wounded at that spot.)

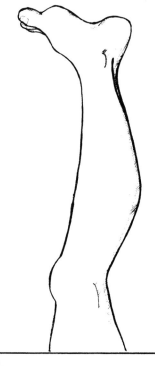

younger. That's one reason why it's important to find sports that you'll continue to enjoy through your whole life.

Flexibility — What's Going On Around the Joint?

Your muscles are anchored to your bones by strong cords of tissue called tendons. These *tendons* pull the bones to make them move around your *joints,* the places where bones connect. Your knees and elbows are two joints. **The part of fitness called flexibility is the amount of movement your bone can make in any direction around a joint.** You need to be flexible to reach for an orange, bend for a penny, or open your mouth in a big yawn.

Your tendons have terrific talents. With flexibility exercises, they can become elastic enough to stretch slowly like a rubber band and yet remain strong enough to pull a weight of nine tons per square inch of tendon. Even then, there are limits to what the most talented tendons can do. With all the neck exercises in the world, teachers can't turn their heads completely around to see who was talking at the back of the room. (You may be glad about that!)

When you do stretching and bending warm-ups before a ball game or a run, you loosen up your tendons the way you would break in a new pair of shoes. You also increase the blood circulation to the parts of your body that you'll be moving. **There's less chance of getting hurt during a game if you stretch your major muscle groups before you start to play.**

Professional athletes do warm-ups before every big game. Baseball players work on preventing leg and shoulder injuries that could result from suddenly moving a stiff muscle. Quarterbacks spend five or ten minutes exercising before a game and during half-time. They do warm-ups so that when they are tackled, their tendons will be better able to absorb the shock.

You start out life amazingly flexible. Babies' feet and hands flop loosely in several directions. But as you get older, it helps to **put a few warm-ups or Yoga stretches into your daily routine** to keep up your stretchability. Before running or getting into an active game, try a few of these runners' warm-ups.

Runners' Warm-Ups

When you run, you give the muscles of your *feet, calves,* and *thighs* an extra work-out. **Before you go out running, stretch these areas so they won't be stiff and possibly get injured.**

Do the stretches slowly. Stretch as far as possible until you get a tight feeling. Hold the stretch for at least ten seconds. After a week or two, increase the time by a few seconds. Don't bounce, or you might tear some muscle fibers.

Repeat each stretch two or three times.

Wall Stretch
(for the muscles in the back of your legs)
1. Stand about 3 feet from a wall, with your legs apart.
2. Place your hands on the wall and lean forward, with arms bent and back straight.
3. Hold for 10 seconds. Do you feel a pull in your legs?

Seat-of-the-Chair Hamstring Stretch
(for the muscles in the back of your legs)
1. Stand near a chair.
2. Lift one leg up onto the seat of the chair and keep it straight. Try to touch the toes of the lifted leg. Hold for 10 seconds.
3. Reverse legs and hold for 10 seconds.

Leg Lift
(for the muscles in the front of your legs)
1. Hold onto a table or chair with one hand.
2. Bend one leg and hold onto that ankle.
3. Pull your ankle slowly behind you. Line up your legs so they're even.
4. Hold for 10 seconds.
5. Switch legs.

Cross-Legged Toe Touch
(for your thighs and back)
1. Cross your legs one way and reach down to touch your toes, keeping your legs straight as you bend forward. Hold for 10 seconds.

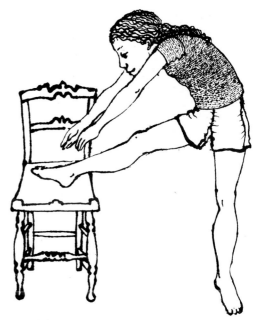

SEAT-OF-THE-CHAIR
HAMSTRING STRETCH

2. Cross your legs the other way and bend forward again. Hold.
3. Repeat 5 times to each side.

Sore Spots

Did you ever give a particular set of muscles such a heavy workout that you felt an ache in that part of the body for a few days? Some exercise scientists say this is because you over-stretched and tore some of the tiny muscle fibers, making you feel pain. The fibers heal quickly, and the aches go away as soon as you get active again. **It's helpful to remember not to strain too much the first time you exercise any muscle group.**

You might also sometimes feel a pain (cramp) in your side when you exercise too soon after a meal. The pain is a sign that more blood is flowing to your digestive organs and less is carrying oxygen to your moving muscles. **To avoid getting cramps, wait at least 45 minutes after you eat before exercising.**

Yoga — Into the Home Stretch

Thousands of years ago in ancient India, people discovered a system of slow and gentle stretching exercises which follow the natural movements of animals, insects, and birds. Today you can follow what they taught. Get yourself into a yoga position that keeps you bent over like a rabbit, balanced on one foot like a stork, or hunched with your head tucked under you like a turtle. **The key is to hold the yoga position for a number of seconds as you breathe deeply and relax.**

Yoga is fun to do anywhere (indoors or out) and any time except right after a meal. With a few minutes of practice each day, you can gradually stretch farther in any yoga position and move on to more difficult ones. At the same time, you increase the blood circulation to different organs, extend and loosen up your tendons, relax your body, and improve how you look and feel. Just remember not to push yourself so far that you feel pain.

Try these yoga poses. They can help keep your back and neck loose.

The Cobra

1. Lie on your stomach, arms at your sides, with palms down, on the floor.
2. Inhale slowly as you raise your head up and arch your back as far as you can. Are there any bugs crawling on the ceiling?
3. Tighten your bottom and thighs. Relax for ten seconds, then lower yourself down as you exhale.

Repeat.

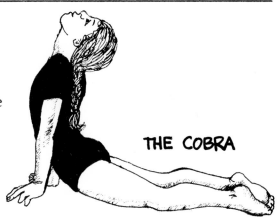

THE COBRA

The Swan (more advanced)

1. Do steps 1 and 2 above.
2. Exhale, and bend your knees, trying to bring your toes toward your head.
3. Hold for 10 to 15 seconds as you breathe normally. With practice, you can bring the two tips of your body closer together.

The Cat Stretch

1. Lie on your stomach, hands at your sides.
2. Place one hand under each shoulder. Breathe in slowly as you push yourself up onto your knees.
3. Hold your breath as you slowly lower your bottom to your heels and your forehead to the floor. S-T-R-E-T-C-H like a cat, from your shoulders to your fingertips. Exhale.
4. Straighten up slowly, bringing your head up last.
5. Sit on your heels. Breathe deeply, in and out.

THE SWAN

THE CAT STRETCH

Your muscles have big appetites, especially when you give them a workout.

In order for muscles to work, they need food and oxygen. The oxygen is used to burn the food within your body. That gives you the energy that keeps you moving.

When you exercise, your body must speedily send extra sugar and oxygen to your muscles to provide extra energy. This is the big over-time delivery job performed by your lungs, heart, and the blood vessels in your body.

The Lungs — Pickup and Delivery

Your lungs are spongy bags of tissue that hang on both sides of your chest cavity. They are made of over 600 million tiny air sacs (alveoli). These air sacs are branched out like grapes on a vine, to make a huge area with tiny blood vessels running through it. If you could spread all your lung tissue out flat, it would cover half a tennis court.

About 15 to 20 times a minute (21,600 times a day) you breathe air in through your nose or mouth, down into your windpipe, and out through the branching bronchial tubes into the millions of air sacs. **The air sacs are like a swap shop for gases in your body.** Oxygen is taken out of the air and absorbed into the blood. Carbon dioxide wastes are taken out of the blood and dumped into the air you exhale.

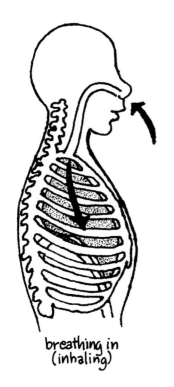

breathing in
(inhaling)

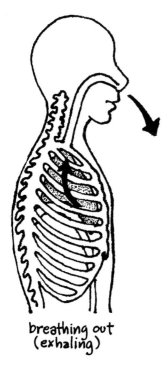

breathing out
(exhaling)

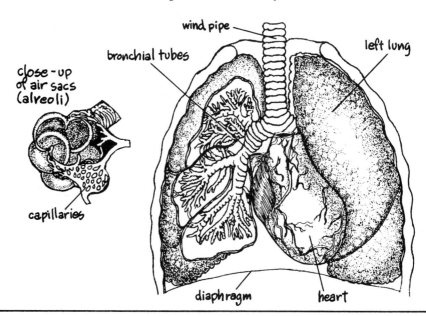

wind pipe

bronchial tubes

left lung

close-up of air sacs (alveoli)

capillaries

diaphragm

heart

Exercise — Speeding Up the Air Flow

When you exercise, the respiratory center in your brain sends a signal that changes your breathing pattern. This signal affects your lungs in two ways:

- You breathe more quickly
- You take deeper breaths each time

The number of breaths you take each minute is called your *breathing rate.* This number decreases as you get older. When you were an infant, you probably breathed 30 to 40 times a minute. By the time you are fully grown, your breathing rate will decrease to about 12 to 15 times a minute. Now your rate is somewhere in between.

The amount of air you normally take in with each breath is called your *breath volume.* (It is also sometimes called your *tidal volume* because your breath flows in and out like the ocean tides.) In any one breath, you never completely fill your lungs. Your breath volume usually fills less than 3/4 of your total *lung capacity,* which is the entire space in your lungs. **Your breath volume goes up during exercise, because your rib muscles and diaphragm work harder to draw in extra air for your moving muscles.**

ONE MINUTE OF BREATHING FOR AN AVERAGE ADULT

	Amount of air in each breath (breath volume)	X	Number of breaths each minute (breathing rate)	=	Total air into lungs each minute
Sitting	½ quart	X	12	=	6 quarts
Jogging	2 quarts	X	40 to 60	=	80 to 120 quarts

Take a look at the One Minute of Breathing Chart. It shows you that **a person can breathe in 17 times more air per minute during exercise (80 to 120 quarts) than at rest (6 quarts).** Athletes may develop such strong rib muscles from active exercise that they can breathe in twice as much air (160 to 220 quarts per minute) during exercise as an average person.

BLOW INTO A BALLOON

In an average day, your lungs move enough air to and fro to blow up over 1,000 party balloons!
How much air can your lungs hold at one time? Test your lung capacity.

1. Blow as much air as you can into a balloon, using just one breath.

2. Compare your balloon's size with that of friends and adults.

Can boys hold more air than girls? Does height make a difference?

Blood Highways — A Round Trip

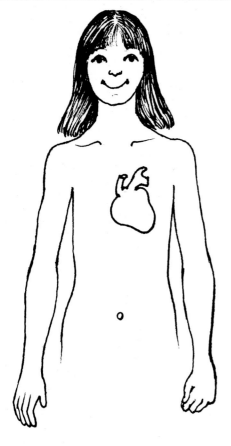

Your body can't store oxygen the way it tucks away food fuel as fat. To keep a constant supply of it moving to the muscles, oxygen must travel through the bloodstream 24 hours every day on hundreds of round trips through the body. Your heart and *circulatory system* make sure the blood moves, so you can move.

Have a Heart!

Your heart is a hollow muscle the size of your fist, sitting right between your lungs, near the center of your body. It pumps 8,000 gallons of blood 12,000 miles throughout your body every day. To do that, it must beat over 100,000 times in 24 hours.

The heart squirts about 1/2 cup of blood through its valves with each heartbeat. The *heart valves* are like gates that open and close to keep the blood flowing in one direction. When you listen to your heart through a *stethoscope,* the beats you hear are the valves slamming shut. Between the beats, the heart relaxes for about half a second. That relaxation is the only cat nap your heart ever gets. When your heart beats fast during exercise, it simply takes shorter rests between the beats.

SQUEEZE PLAY

Fold one hand over the other and keep squeezing it 80 times in one minute. Could you do that for 1,440 minutes in a row without getting tired?

That's how hard your heart works every day of your life.

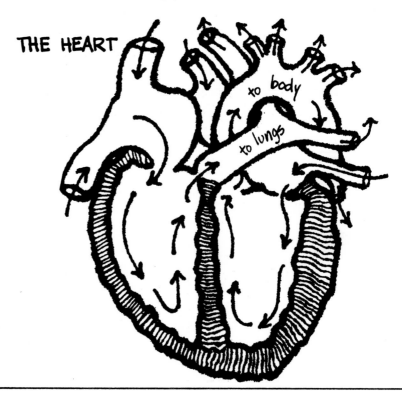

THE HEART

to body

to lungs

Traveling Through the Tubes

Oxygen-rich blood is pumped by your heart into tubes that lead to your arms and legs and the organs of your body. These tubes are called *arteries.* The arteries split into tiny blood vessels called *capillaries* (the word capillary comes from the Latin word for hair). You could fit 100 capillaries side by side on the period at the end of this sentence.

The capillaries supply the oxygen the muscles need for movement. They are also waste pick-up places. They carry away the carbon dioxide and other waste products that the muscles make when they burn food for energy. Capillaries lead from the muscles and organs into bigger and bigger blood vessels called *veins.* The veins collect blood from all over the body and return it to the heart. The entire trip from the heart to the muscles and back again takes less than a minute.

The heart pumps the blood which no longer has much oxygen back to the lungs for a fresh supply. Then the oxygen pick-up and waste drop-off cycle begins all over again.

Feeding the Master Muscle

Your heart needs oxygen, too, to produce energy for its constant pumping action. **The heart muscle is so thick that it needs its own system of arteries and capillaries.** The coronary (heart) arteries are straw-sized tubes that act like your heart's lifeline. When people have a heart attack, it usually means that one of these coronary arteries has become blocked and can no longer deliver its share of oxygen to part of the heart.

THE CIRCULATORY SYSTEM

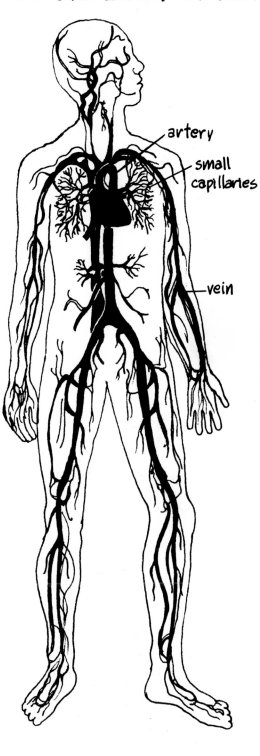

artery

small capillaries

vein

THE HEART

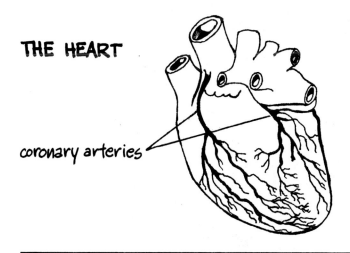

coronary arteries

Heartbeats and Pulse Beats

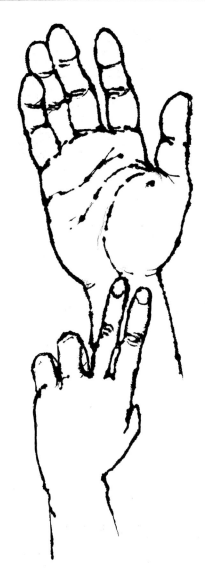

PICK A PULSE POINT

How many pulse points can you find on your own body? Tip: run in place for half a minute before you try to find them.
(See page 210 for the answer)

The Heart Facts of Life

- Your heart started beating 6 months before you were born. During an average lifetime, it will beat almost 3 billion times.
- If you weigh 100 pounds, you have a little less than one pound of heart and seven pounds of blood, enough to fill four quart-size milk cartons.
- Your blood makes 1,000 complete trips around your body each day. Each trip takes less than one minute.
- In a lifetime, your heart might pump 77 million gallons of blood. That would fill all the tanks in the New England Aquarium 150 times.
- Your blood contains about 25 trillion *red blood cells* that transport oxygen to your muscles and organs. About 8 million of them die every second and are replaced by new ones.

Your Pulse — Picking Up the Beat

When the heart contracts (pumps), it forces blood out into the arteries. The walls of the arteries stretch. As the heart relaxes, the artery walls contract to push the blood along. **Each time the artery walls expand and contract is one pulse beat.**

You can feel the pulse beats of your arteries at special pulse points on your body where the arteries are close to the surface. Your pulse rate is the number of times you feel a beat each minute. **The resting pulse rate for most healthy 11-year-olds is somewhere between 70 and 100 beats per minute.** For an average adult, it is around 60 to 80 beats per minute.

Your pulse feels strong and regular when you are healthy and may be weak when you are sick. That's one reason why doctors and nurses take a patient's pulse.

Downbeat

A person's resting pulse rate decreases with age.

Newborn baby — 130 to 150 beats each minute
1-year-old — about 100 to 130 beats each minute
6-year-old — about 90 to 110 beats each minute
11-year-old — about 70 to 100 beats each minute
Adult — about 60 to 80 beats each minute

These are all *average* rates. Some very fit people have rates as low as 45 beats per minute, and healthy 10-year-olds can have heart rates of 110, or even more.

Pulse Practice

Run in place for 30 seconds. Then locate the pulse point on the inside of your left wrist, between the bone and tendon on your thumb side. You can find another pulse point on your neck on the left or right side of the windpipe.

Place three fingers lightly on the spot. Use a watch with a second hand. Count the number of beats you feel in 15 seconds. Multiply this number by four to get your resting pulse rate for one minute. Try it twice. Do you get the same results each time?

Now that you've mastered the basics, test out some pulse rate changes when your body is in different situations.

Take your pulse —
• Before you get out of bed in the morning.
• After you eat a big meal.
• When you are sitting and relaxing.
• When you feel excited or tense.
• After running or doing exercises for a few minutes.

Can you think of other activities that might affect your pulse? If you want to get a *real* resting pulse rate, you might ask your parents to take your pulse while you are asleep.

Keep a chart of your results. Compare it with what your friends find.

PULSE PRACTICE

	Pulse rate for 15 seconds	X 4 =	Pulse rate per minute
Trial 1		X 4 =	
Trial 2		X 4 =	

Pulse Rate	Situation
90	Just finished dinner
80	Did a yoga "cat" stretch

Size Them Up

Fitness level, age, and size are some reasons why a person's pulse rate may be high or low. Generally, larger people have a slightly lower pulse rate.

Look at this sample of resting pulse rates of different animals. Does size seem to make a difference here?

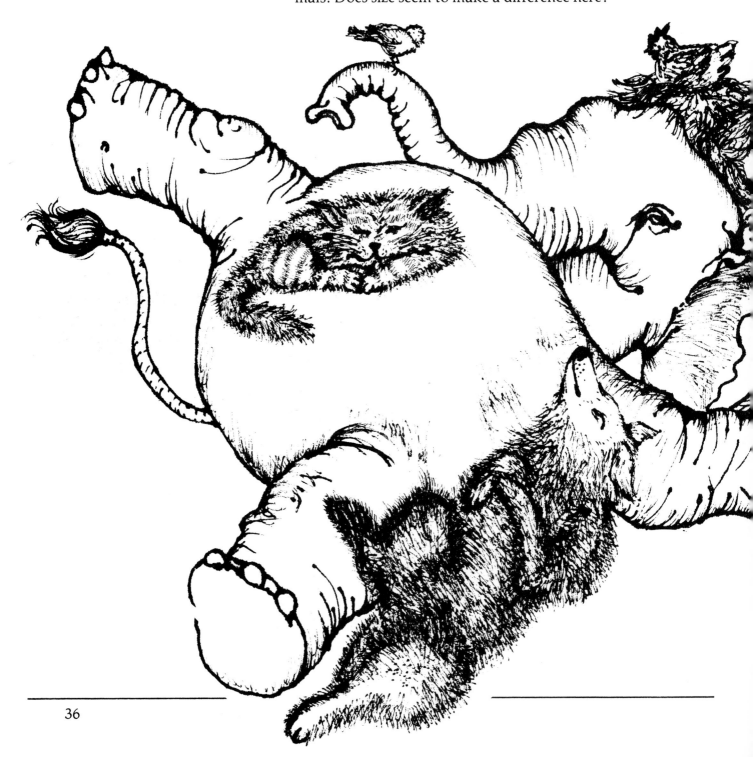

Do you know two animals of different sizes (including humans) whose pulse rates you can check to see the difference?

All these animals have hearts that will beat about 1 billion times in a lifetime. Which animals do you think live longer — canaries or elephants?

The only exception is man. Our hearts are good for over 2½ billion beats in a lifetime of 70 years. Some people believe that if you could make your heart beat less often, you might spread these heartbeats over a longer lifetime.

RESTING PULSE BEATS PER MINUTE

Canary	500 to 800
Mouse	300 to 500
Chicken	300 to 350
Cat	120 to 140
Dog	70 to 120
Person	60 to 80
Lion	40 to 50
Elephant	25 to 50

What happens to a strong heart and lungs team if an enemy moves in? Suppose an active, healthy person begins to smoke. It's surprising how quickly smoking limits that person's ability to move fast and stay active for a long time. **Smoking makes the heart and lungs work less efficiently,** and many smokers can feel these effects whenever they move around.

When people bring a foreign substance like cigarette smoke into their bodies, they invite in a swarm of over 2,000 chemicals, including small quantities of the poisons *tar, nicotine,* and *carbon monoxide.* These chemicals have immediate effects on the heart, blood, and lungs.

The Heart and Blood Vessels

The nicotine in cigarettes speeds up the heartbeat by 10 to 20 beats each minute. At the same time, it makes the arteries narrower. This means that less blood flows through the arteries to the muscles although the heart is beating more rapidly than usual. **So smokers may get tired more quickly.**

The carbon monoxide in cigarettes latches onto the *hemoglobin* in your red blood cells 250 times faster than oxygen can. This means that the red blood cells can't carry as much oxygen as they normally would. **Smokers may have to breathe harder to get the same amount of oxygen delivered to the muscles.** Have you ever watched a heavy smoker pant for breath as he/she climbed a long flight of stairs?

The Lungs

When a person breathes in cigarette smoke, the tar remains inside his/her air passageways and paralyzes the *cilia.* Cilia are millions of tiny hairs that line the inside of your windpipe and bronchial tubes. They sweep out any dirt and germs that you breathe in. A single cigarette can stop cilia from moving for 20 minutes or more. **When the cilia aren't able to do their job for a long time, a smoker has to cough a lot to get the mucus and dirt out of his/her lungs.**

If this continues to happen over many years, a serious illness called *bronchitis* may develop, where a person is forced to cough constantly to keep lungs clean. When smokers give up cigarettes, they can repair much of the damage to the cilia.

Healthy lung tissue is made up of spongy sacs of air. The tar and nicotine in cigarettes can scar and break the tiny air sacs, leaving big gaping air pockets. Breathing becomes more and more difficult, and eventually a disease called *emphysema* may develop. People who have severe emphysema can't breathe well enough to lead normal lives. They may have to spend their last years unable to work, play, or even walk across a room. This is one condition that does *not* disappear after smokers give up the habit.

Smoking Statistics: Sad Signs

- Today there are about 50 million smokers in the U.S.
- Over 500 billion cigarettes are sold here yearly.
- The average smoker spends about $300 a year on cigarettes.
- There are almost 5 million teenagers who smoke. The number of teen-age girls who smoke is rising faster than any other group of Americans.

Hopeful Signs

- A big anti-smoking movement has started and is spreading.
- In 1971, the government banned all cigarette commercials on radio and TV.
- In the past five years, there are more limits on places where people can smoke, fewer cigarette vending machines, more quit-smoking clinics, and special non-smoking sections in restaurants, planes, trains, and stores.
- Thirty million people in the U.S. have quit smoking. Today, 2/3 of the American population do *not* smoke.

Why Start?

If smoking does all this damage, why do some people, especially kids, try cigarettes and then continue to smoke them? They may think it makes them look cool and grown-up, or be afraid they'll be called "chicken" by their smoking friends if they say no. Some kids feel more popular when they copy what their friends are doing. And some kids who already smoke put pressure on other kids to try it. There may be some-

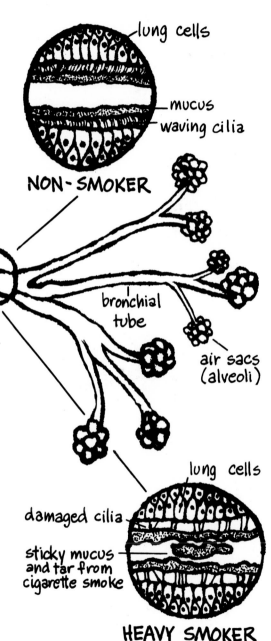

INSIDE THE BRONCHIAL TUBES

lung cells

mucus

waving cilia

NON-SMOKER

bronchial tube

air sacs (alveoli)

lung cells

damaged cilia

sticky mucus and tar from cigarette smoke

HEAVY SMOKER

BE SMART. DON'T START

Write a slogan, ad, or poster to convince people not to smoke. Give health reasons or social reasons. Here are some slogans that are being used today:

"You smoke, I choke."

"Don't be an ash."

"Don't smoke, you'll croak."

"Smokers are air polluters."

"Puffers will suffer."

WARNING: The surgeon general has determined that cigarette smoking is dangerous to your health.

one in your family who smokes or has quit smoking, and this may influence the choices you make, too.

Adults and young people who smoke often started because of advertising campaigns that told them smoking would be fun, make them attractive, or give them special pleasure. The tobacco industry spends over $250 million on advertisements for cigarettes each year. What are some of the messages they bring you?

- Be a rugged outdoors person.
- Feel cool, relaxed, and refreshed.
- Lower tar and nicotine levels mean this cigarette won't hurt you as much.
- Liberated women choose this brand.

Can you think of other appeals cigarette ads make? What would an honest advertisement tell you about smoking?

It's often very difficult for smokers to stop, even when they want to. This is because cigarette smoking can become an automatic habit that people do without thinking. Some people reach for a cigarette whenever they feel tense. Cigarettes don't give them much relief, though, because they speed up the heart rate instead of slowing it down. Some people smoke because they don't want to gain weight. (Old Lucky Strike cigarette advertisements used to tell people, "Reach for a Lucky instead of a sweet." That ad sold billions of cigarettes!) Other people smoke when they are lonely, angry, or just want to have something to do. For whatever reasons people smoke, they often get addicted to cigarettes and find it really hard to quit.

Calling It Quits

Today there is more pressure for people to stop smoking than ever before from the 2/3 of the American public who *don't* smoke. **Many non-smokers don't want to breathe in smoke from other people's cigarettes.** It can pollute the air in a room as much as a factory can pollute the air in a city.

Smoke from another person's cigarette is called "second-hand smoke." It contains large quantities of the odorless, colorless poison carbon monoxide which causes eye irritations and breathing difficulties. If you inhale "second-hand smoke," your heart beats faster and your blood pressure goes up. Did you

know that lung illnesses are twice as common in young kids with parents who smoke at home as in kids with non-smoking parents?

Many non-smokers are asking the government to limit the places where people can smoke, and to make smokers pay fines if they break the law. Some people don't keep ashtrays in their homes, or will ask smokers to put out their cigarettes. And thousands of smokers themselves are quitting, either alone or by joining anti-smoking groups.

One of the biggest reasons for quitting today is the big interest in fitness. Smokers often give up cigarettes once they start jogging or playing sports regularly. They find that exercise can be a "positive addiction" that takes the place of a harmful habit like smoking.

LUNGS
AT WORK—
NO SMOKING

AN EX-SMOKER SPEAKS

Interview a person who has quit smoking.

How did he/she start? How many cigarettes did he/she smoke each day? How much money was spent on cigarettes each week? (Figure out the total for one year.) Did smoking cause any problems?

You are jogging around the track at a comfortable pace. What is the inside story of your run?

- Your arm, shoulder, and leg muscles are contracting and relaxing quickly, burning up fuel energy as they go.

- Your heart muscle is squeezing and pumping blood to all parts of the body at about 140 to 170 beats per minute. Up to eight times more blood is being pumped each minute than when you are resting.

- More blood is being sent to the arms and legs where it is most needed. Less of it is flowing to the digestive organs like the stomach and intestines.

- Your rib cage is expanding and contracting over 40 times a minute, as your lungs breathe in over 50 quarts of air. You are breathing rhythmically and deeply as you run.

Most physically-fit 11-year-olds could keep up this slow and steady jogging pace for 15 to 20 minutes at a time. Do you think they could keep up a *fast* run for a full 20 minutes?

Aerobic Exercise — Going Steady

Think of how a flashbulb compares to a lamp you plug into a wall. One gives you extra-bright light for a quick moment and fizzles out, the other uses electric power to glow steadily. Your body also provides two different kinds of energy — one for the activities you do in a flash, like the 100-yard dash, and the other for activities that keep you moving steadily for five minutes or more, like a jog or a long bike ride.

The dash is over so quickly that it doesn't require much energy. You can rely on a small amount of energy that the muscles produce quickly without using any new supplies of oxygen. This is called *anaerobic* energy. ("An" means without and "aerobic" means using oxygen.) Because this energy supply is limited, you can rely on your anaerobic system only for activities that take less than a couple of minutes. After that, you must begin to use your jogging type of energy, called *aerobic* energy.

Aerobic activities are exercises and sports that usually take five minutes or more and keep you breathing deeply so you can bring in more oxygen for your moving muscles. They don't require fast movements that would quickly tire you or leave you out of breath.

The Aerobic Training Effect

Swimming, jogging, fast walking, or biking three or four times a week helps keep you fit by making your heart, diaphragm, and rib muscles stronger. This important part of fitness is called heart and lung endurance, or — the fancy word for it — cardio-respiratory endurance. ("Cardio" means relating to the heart, and "respiratory" means relating to breathing.)

Remember how placing an extra load on a muscle over a long period of time makes it stronger? You place a continuous extra load on your heart and chest muscles when you do regular aerobic exercise. Your heart, diaphragm, and rib muscle fibers grow larger, and new capillaries open up, bringing in extra oxygen. Then, even when you aren't exercising, you benefit from the aerobic training effect:

- You breathe in more air with each breath (higher breath volume).
- Your heart pumps extra blood with each heartbeat (higher stroke volume).

People who do aerobic exercise several times a week develop very strong heart muscles. Strong hearts don't need to beat as fast to deliver the same amount of blood. This means that fit people often have low heart rates. That saves their hearts a lot of work. If you could cut your heart rate by 10 to 15 beats each minute, you would save 15,000 to 20,000 beats a day, or more than 7 million beats a year.

STROKE VOLUME

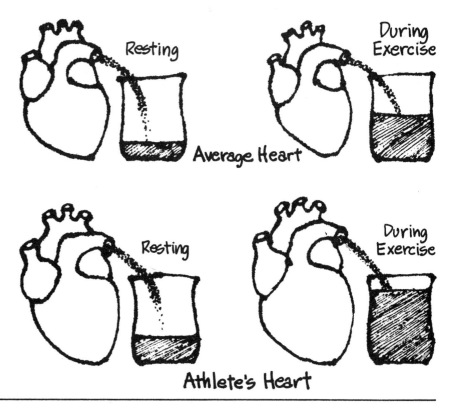

Resting

During Exercise

Average Heart

Resting

During Exercise

Athlete's Heart

Getting On Target

How do you know when the exercise you are doing is aerobic? Exercise scientists have figured out ways to measure the very highest rate at which our hearts can beat. This rate, called the *maximum heart rate,* is different for different people, depending on their age, size, and how fit or unfit they are. For most 10- to 12-year-olds, the maximum heart rate is about 200 beats each minute.

You are really exercising your heart if you get your pulse rate up to about 3/4 of your maximum heart rate. That is your *target zone* for an aerobic exercise program. **For most 10- to 12-year-olds, the target zone is about 140 to 170 beats each minute.** After you jog, swim, or bike in your target zone a few times, you won't need to take your pulse to know how it feels for you to move at that rate.

After a month or two of regular aerobic exercise, your pulse will return to its resting rate more quickly when you finish exercising. You then have a faster *pulse recovery.* Why is there a change? Since your heart gets stronger from aerobic activities, it doesn't need to beat as fast when you are exercising. So it can come down to its resting rate sooner.

If your heart takes less than 45 seconds to get back to its resting rate after five or ten minutes of aerobic activity, you're in good shape.

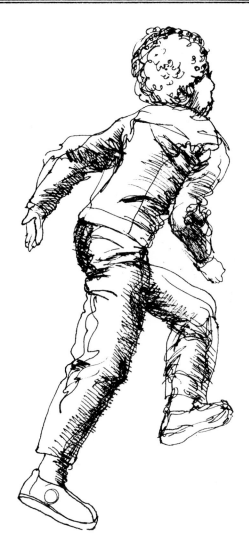

MY AEROBIC ACTIVITY PLAN
* CONTRACT *

I, _____
promise myself to complete
_____ weeks of aerobic
training, at least three
times a week, from

until _____.

The activities I plan to do
are:

_____
_____
_____
_____
_____
_____

_____
Name

There are many activities that can be aerobic if you move continuously so that your pulse rate reaches your target zone: basketball, biking, disco-dancing, folk and square dancing, hiking, jogging, skating, snow-shoeing, cross-country skiing, swimming (the crawl), tag games, and walking (briskly).

How can you build more aerobic activity into your lifestyle? Sometimes you can find a fitness group to join. Does your school have a morning running or an after-school sports program? Do you have a friend or two who would also like to run, bike, or swim? Would anyone in your family join you? A regular aerobic program is easier to stick to if there are a few people doing it together.

Make a plan for yourself for the coming month. Set aside 30 minutes three days a week for warm-ups, your aerobic activity, and cooling down. On some days you might like to have two 15-minute sessions, one in the morning and one in the afternoon. Leave at least one rest day between every two exercise days. Choose a few different activities or stick with one you really love to do. One way you can hold yourself to your plan is to write yourself a contract and put it up where you can see it every day.

A Travel Log to Timbuktu

Aerobic activities can get you places. How far can you go in one or two months' time?

1. Think of a place you'd like to visit, like a park, a museum, or a nearby city.
2. Use a map to figure out how many miles it is from where you live.
3. Measure some routes you can jog, fast-walk, or bike a few times a week (to and from school, the supermarket, your best friend's house, a church or temple).
4. For one month, try to cover as much distance as you can aerobically on your routes.
5. Keep a travel log and mark off the quarter miles toward your goal as you cover them.

Goal: Grandma's house
Distance: 20 miles

home   Grandma's house

| 1 | 2 | 3 | 4 | 5 | 6 | 7 | 8 | 9 | 10 | 11 | 12 | 13 | 14 | 15 | 16 | 17 | 18 | 19 | 20 | miles |

When you reach your goal, give yourself a reward. Maybe you can even visit that place with your family.

If your friends or classmates are keeping travel logs, add up your mileage together for a group travel log. Keep track of the distances you all cover each week by moving a colored tack across a map. Can you make it to a different city in a week? A different state in a month? A different country by the end of the school year?

Run for Your Life

Over 2,000 years ago, in Greece, a messenger ran over twenty miles from the battlefield on the Plains of Marathon to the city of Athens to tell the people their army had crushed the invaders from Persia. As soon as he got the words out of his mouth, he dropped dead from exhaustion! That was the world's first marathon run.

The Boston Marathon began in 1897 as a race for amateurs who enjoyed running and wanted to see how far they could push their bodies to complete a long endurance feat. In 1979, over 7,500 runners entered the 26½ mile race held in mid-April on Patriots' Day. Crowds of more than 250,000 turned out to see how they ran. The leader was Bill Rodgers, a three-time winner, who set a new marathon record of 2 hours, 9 minutes, and 27 seconds.

MR. MARATHON

Clarence DeMar was one of the most famous Boston Marathon runners. He was born in 1890 with a curved spine that made it hard for him even to walk when he was very

young. When he was 8 years old, his father died, and he had to go to work to help his mother provide for his five sisters and brothers. He ran up and down hilly roads selling sewing goods door to door, moving with an awkward shuffle because of his handicap.

Later on in college, DeMar took jobs on a farm and at a print shop, and ran from one to the other for a total of eight miles a day. In spite of his odd way of running, he could move very quickly over long distances.

Friends encouraged DeMar to train for the Boston Marathon. In 1911, he entered the race and set a new record, finishing in 2 hours, 21 minutes, and 39 seconds. He later went on to win the Marathon seven times, and he completed more than 1,000 long-distance races, including the International Olympics Marathon which he ran at the age of 36!

He continued to run for enjoyment until he was almost 70. When DeMar died, doctors were amazed to find that the arteries around his heart were three times the normal size from his lifetime of aerobic exercise.

AEROBIC KICKS

Imagine kicking a ball around for two full days non-stop, covering 100 to 200 miles of hilly countryside as you move. Sound impossible? The Tarahumara Indians of Mexico often run that kind of continuous kick-ball relay race just for fun. They stay in shape for it by running every day in the mountains where they live. After years of that kind of lifestyle, it's no wonder the Tarahumaras are considered the greatest endurance runners in the world.

A Running Start

If you're ready to give yourself a run-around, jogging is a good way to start. Jogging is actually slow running over a medium to long distance. A few tips before you begin:

- Do runners' warm-ups beforehand. (See page 27.) Start by jogging very slowly and cool down with a few minutes of slow jogging in the end.

- Wear running shoes. They give your foot muscles the support they need. Try to run on a track or on a firm, grassy area.

- Breathe in deeply with your mouth open. Don't go so fast that you can't talk as you run.

- If you feel pain or get out of breath, slow down. Walk until you feel ready to run again.

- Keep your back straight, chin up, and arms bent at the elbows.

- The first few times out, take your pulse sometime during the jog. Are you in your target zone? After that, you'll know how it feels to be jogging at a good pace for you.

Aer-Rope-Ics

Feeling jumpy? Set a personal record by jumping longer each time you jump rope. Rope jumping has been a favorite activity all over the world for hundreds of years. Cherokee

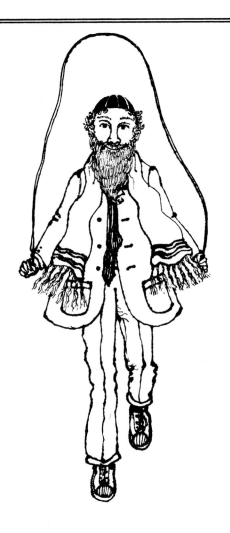

JUMP TO A JINGLE

Annie, cumbanny,
Tee alligo skanny.
T-legged
Tie-legged
Bow-legged Annie.

Indians used to jump over grape vines, and people in Hungary used to skip over long pieces of straw. Today, wrestlers and tennis pros jump rope to build their arm strength as well as their heart and lung endurance.

Who holds the world rope-jumping record? In 1976, a rabbi in Milwaukee went 50,000 turns without stopping!

Remember the overload principle as you plan an aerobic jump rope program. Do more jumps or take fewer rests each time out. For example, you might begin with 50 jumps and a rest of 15 counts. Then start again for another 50, and rest for 15 counts again. In a few days' time, rest for only 10 counts, then only 5. Can you get beyond 150 jumps non-stop? What is your record for jumps with a rest? What is your record for hot peppers?

Variety is the spice of rope-jumping. Do you know any jump rope jingles? Try jumping to music.

Do special steps as you jump. Make up a special pattern using skips, hops, backward rope turning, crossed-hands, crossed-leg jumps, straddle jumps, toe-taps, and other fancy steps. Do a certain number of jumps in one style, then switch to another. Jump slowly, then do hot peppers.

You're All Wet

Get into the swim of things. If there's a pool nearby, you can use it regularly for your aerobic fitness program. The crawl and back crawl can be great exercise for all the major muscles of your body, as well as for your heart and lungs. Swim as many laps as you can without stopping. Can you get in good enough shape to swim for five minutes or more at a stretch?

If you'd like to increase your flexibility, try some water exercises. Many are just like the ones you do on land (sit-ups are tough to do in water, though!) The extra push of the water against your muscles does even more to build your muscle strength and endurance. For example, try kicks as you hold the side of the pool, jog in waist-level water, or walk in a crouched position where it's very shallow. Water games like "Marco Polo" or Water Tag are fun ways to keep active and build aerobic fitness.

Like to Bike?

Build up your biking abilities. Bike faster for a short distance, then go back to your regular rate. Bike along a flat stretch, then a hilly area for 10 minutes or more, then a flat stretch again. In that way, you'll get some aerobic benefit.

Are there any bike paths near where you live? There are now about 16,000 miles of special bikeways in the U.S. Many more thousands of miles of bike paths are being built as the bicycling boom spreads.

Two wheels can sometimes even get you places faster than four. During a contest in San Francisco, one man took 31 minutes to get through the city traffic by car. The other man crossed the city in only 19 minutes by bike!

SPINNING WHEELS

What's the farthest you've ever biked in one day? Did you know that distance bike racers in Europe can cover up to 150 miles a day for three weeks, going an average of 20 to 25 miles per-hour on flat stretches? Every year 15 million spectators line the roads in France to watch about 100 cyclists go by at that rate during the *Tour de France* races. Racing bicyclists are big heroes in France, like baseball, hockey, and football players in America. In fact, the *Tour de France* is called the World Series of bicycle races.

DANCING THE WEEKS AWAY

In 1928, the "Dance Derby of the Century" was held in Madison Square Garden in New York City. Hundreds of couples from all over the country entered the competition, including some prize-winning runners, swimmers, and pedestrians (distance walkers). Everyone wanted to break the old dancing records and get the $5,000 prize.

Once the contest began, each couple was allowed only 15 minutes each hour for eating and resting. The first couple dropped out after two and a half hours. One week later, only 28 couples were left. Some snoozed on each other's shoulders, which was allowed as long as their feet never stopped moving. The contest finally ended 481 dancing hours later, after two weeks and six days of straight dancing!

The Marathon dancers didn't move fast enough to dance aerobically, but you can. You don't have to break any records at the Hustle, the Freak, or the Funky Chicken to dance your way to greater flexibility and fitness. Do folk dances in the gym or disco dances to your favorite records at home. Keep moving steadily to get your heart rate up. _____

New Ways to Play

A lot of people in the United States are getting interested in games that many people can play without having to beat another person or another team. These are called *cooperative* games.

Sometimes the rules for old games can be changed so people work together instead of against each other. Volleyball can be scored according to how many times *both* teams get the ball over the net before it hits the ground. In cooperative dodgeball games, you keep changing sides or add points to the *other* team's total each time you score. In some cooperative games, dozens of people work together to become a human pyramid, toss a frisbee, or push a giant ball around the field.

One 10-year-old invented a cooperative game where "It" is a snake crawling in the grass. Anyone who gets touched has to

GUESS-TIMATING

Next time you and a friend are doing an aerobic activity like running, swimming, or biking, try "guess-timating." Predict the time it will take for each of you to complete a distance. How close do your predictions come to the real time? Try to make your "guess-timates" closer as you get to know yourselves better.

crawl like a snake too. The game continues until everyone is a snake. Can you think of any ways to make your favorite games more cooperative? How about thinking up new ways to play tag?

TAG-GET FIT CHASING "IT"

A thousand years ago in Europe, people of all ages used to believe in invisible spirits like demons, witches, goblins, wizards, dybbuks, and fairies. They tried to avoid evil spells by running to a safe place or touching certain objects made of iron or wood. Squatting down to mumble a prayer might also drive the demons away. If "It" was after you, you'd simply have to escape by heading in the opposite direction or doing something to make you safe.

Does this sound familiar? You may have played tag since you were little without knowing you were running away from invisible spirits. Today, there are many tags games based on the old iron, wood, or squat tag games of the olden days. Try a few like Hugging Tag to stay on the move.

HUGGING TAG
Play a game of tag where the only way a player is safe is by hugging (or holding) another player. After playing a while, change the rules so three people must hug each other to be safe from "It." Togetherness pays!

Girls and Boys on the Go

Do you know boys who take ballet lessons? Are there girls on the Little League teams in your neighborhood? Male dancers and female baseball players may be easy to find nowadays, but years ago things were different.

For thousands of years, activities like swimming, archery, and wrestling were ways boys learned skills they needed as adults to hunt, fight in wars, or protect their families. They would train for months and then compete against the other boys of their age at community sports events. That was one way to show their tribe or village how much they had learned.

Girls, on the other hand, were expected to stay home and take care of the house and family. They were not allowed to take part in any organized games, so they never had a chance to develop athletic skills.

Two thousand years ago in Greece, women were banned from participating in the Olympics. They were sentenced to death if they were caught even watching the games! Times have changed. In 1976, nearly half the Olympic participants were women. Many of them are now beating past men's records in gymnastics, swimming, track and field, and distance running.

People used to think that sports were not "ladylike," or were too difficult for females to play well. Proper young women in the 1800's were told to stick with quiet sports like "gentle" tennis or badminton, archery, and riding side-saddle on a walking horse. Girls could take part only in games where they could wear long dresses and not get too sweaty. How would you feel if you had to play soccer or tennis in a long skirt?

Some people still think that boys and girls have very different abilities which limit sports they should play. What are the facts?

Until the age of 12 or 13, boys and girls are about equal in terms of speed, strength, and endurance. Extra male hormones are produced during boys' teen-age growth spurts. This gives them larger muscles which add arm and shoulder strength. This added strength matters the most in body contact sports like football, wrestling, and weightlifting. Teen-aged boys also develop broader shoulders which help them throw a ball farther than most girls. But girls are generally more flexible. They have equal endurance and plenty of leg strength for long-distance running, swimming, and skiing.

In championship tennis, gymnastics, or track and field events, muscular strength in the arms may count for a lot. It is probably fairer for people of the same sex to compete with each other. But for the games you play with friends, your muscle strength and the width of your shoulders don't matter much. You can always find boys and girls who enjoy playing the same sports as you do and who play at your level.

MARATHON MISS-TAKE

In 1967, a woman named Kathy Switzer decided to run in the all-male Boston Marathon. She sent in an application signed "K. Switzer." On the day of the race, she wore a hooded sweatshirt to hide her identity.

Once the running began, the hood came off her head. After that, the news spread quickly — K. Switzer was *not* a Kevin, or a Kenneth! The director of the Marathon tried to throw her out, but her male running companion pushed him aside so Kathy could finish the race.

It wasn't until 1972 that women could officially enter the Boston Marathon. By 1979, 517 women finished the race, proof of the endurance abilities and growing fitness interest of many women. Today, women are off and running in races all over the country.

Only about five years ago, some 9- and 10-year-old girls went to court for the right to join their local Little League team. They won their case and made it possible for girls all over the country to play baseball today. In 1972, a new law stated that schools must provide an equal chance for both boys and girls to participate in school sports. That's one reason why girls' participation in basketball, track and field, swimming, and volleyball has more than doubled in the past two years.

Many males are trying out activities that used to be considered feminine. More boys than ever before are dancing, doing yoga, or learning new skills in gymnastics and skating. These are physical activities that take years of fitness training and practice to do well. In fact, few sports require the endurance, flexibility, and strength of ballet.

NUREYEV LEAPS - AND BALLET BOOMS

Why is there a growing interest in male ballet dancing? The 40-year-old Russian-born ballet star Rudolf Nureyev has a lot to do with it. Ever since he began to dance in Europe and America in 1961, audiences have been amazed by the breathtaking leaps and turns of male ballet stars. There are about 15 million ballet fans in America today.

Nureyev's leaps don't just happen. He has trained for many years to build up his leg strength and his flexibility. He came from a poor family that couldn't afford to send him to the city for dance lessons. So he began by folk dancing with a

group that went from town to town. When he performed at a folk festival in Moscow, a ballet teacher saw him and offered him a scholarship at the most famous ballet school in the country. From then on, Nureyev worked day in and day out, six to eight hours a day, to become the greatest dance star in Russia and then the world.

Nureyev has the cardio-respiratory and muscle endurance to dance for hours and do 48 performances in 47 days. He says, "I can't sit. I must dance." He has danced with every important dance company in the world. And today, the number of boys following in Nureyev's footsteps is growing by leaps and bounds.

Your Fitness Guide

Look ahead to the ways you can get into better shape this coming month. What are the active games you enjoy playing most? Do you know how they may be keeping you fit? Check the Fitness Scoresheet on the next page to see which ways the games you play help keep your body in shape.

The exact amount of exercise you need to stay in shape is an individual thing. However, you can keep in mind some handy guides.

- Remember the overload principle. Start slowly and set goals for yourself that you try to reach as you exercise more. The key is to increase how hard, how often, or how long you play a game or work on a skill.
- Start each aerobic activity with some warm-ups, like bending and stretching, slow jogging, and practicing a few of the skills you'll use in the game. Get ready from head to toe, and you'll be a lot less likely to feel sore later.
- Get into a routine. Set aside certain parts of the day or the week for aerobics. Don't leave it only for the weekends.
- Try out a variety of activities. That helps you have more fun staying active.
- Exercise with a friend.
- Reward yourself for a job well done.

Set up a contract or performance test so you know how much progress you have made. Time yourself and break your old records. Check your resting and exercise pulse rate a few months after you start to get in shape, and see if there are any changes.

FITNESS SCORESHEET

	Cardio-Respiratory Endurance (Aerobic Fitness)	Muscular Endurance	Muscular Strength	Flexibility
Jogging or Running	**	**	**	✓
Bicycling	**	**	**	✓
Swimming (crawl)	**	**	**	**
Skating (ice or roller skating)	**	**	**	*
Skiing (cross-country)	**	**	**	*
Skiing (downhill)	*	**	**	*
Basketball	**	**	**	*
Gymnastics and Warm-ups	✓	*	**	**
Walking fast	*	*	*	*
Soccer	*	**	*	✓
Softball	—	✓	✓	✓
Bowling	—	—	—	✓

This scoring system shows the way different activities help you stay fit.

Scores: ** = Very high benefit   * = High benefit   ✓ = Some benefit   — = Low benefit

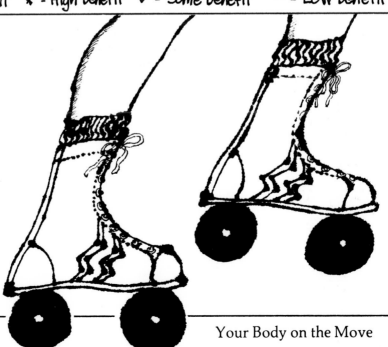

LISTENING TO YOUR BODY

Variety

GIVE YOUR FRIEND A HAND!

Get together with a group of friends. Ask them to take a close look at their hands, and to write a description of one of them. Now mix the papers up and see if you can match each hand with its description.

Did you ever look closely at an apple picked ripe off a tree? If you did, you might have noticed that its size, shape, and color were different from all the other fruits that grew on the same tree.

We humans are also home-grown products of nature, each one different from the rest. The fruits and vegetables you see on display in a supermarket have been specially grown so they all have the same good looks or tough skins. But we humans are like the vegetables you grow in your garden, not identical supermarket vegetables. In fact, it's our natural variety that makes us all so interesting.

MY FAVORITE THINGS

Make a list of the things you like best about yourself: how you look, how you do things, and how you use your special talents.

You may not always appreciate the ways in which you look different from other people. Perhaps you carry around a picture of yourself inside your head which you keep comparing with photos of TV stars, athletes, models, or the friends you admire. That inside picture is your *self-image*. A lot of people want to change their self-image to fit some ideal. They aren't always happy with the way they look and feel. Whenever *you* get the urge to be like someone else, think about the things that make you special.

What's Beautiful?

Our ideas of beauty keep changing, like clothing fashions and car models that go in and out of style.

- A few hundred years ago, artists looked for plump female models to put in their paintings to fit their idea of beauty.

- Long hair, moustaches, and beards for men have been in and out of fashion since Biblical days. Who knows what will happen to men's hair styles next?

- In the late 1800's, ladies used to struggle into tightly laced corsets to get a "wasp waist" figure. They may have looked like hourglasses, but they couldn't breathe properly and often fainted from too much activity.

- People used to think that a fat baby was always a very healthy baby. In some countries of Europe and Asia, mothers gave their infants special charms to help them gain weight.

Make-Over Magic

Will a prince on a white horse charge up to your doorstep once you try Speckles Anti-Dandruff Shampoo? Will the girls fight for a whiff of your Rose Petals mouthwash or Arm Charm deodorant? Maybe not, but TV commercials can get you hooked on their products by selling you these wild dreams. Cosmetics companies spend over $500 million a year on advertisement fantasies to convince you to cover up your face, hide your natural body odor, freshen your breath, or add color to your hair, eyes, cheeks, and lips.

MAKE-OVER MESSAGES

Look closely at magazine ads and TV commercials. Make a list of advertised products that people use to change their appearance. What are some of the reasons why people buy them?

What's the impact of these make-over messages? **Americans spend over $8 billion each year buying beauty products,** including over $25 million on dandruff "cures," $400 million on deodorants, and $60 million on suntan lotions and oils. Ten out of every hundred Americans change the color of their hair, and they spend $250 million doing it. While some women curl their hair, others straighten it, and men with thinning hair buy hair creams or toupees. There are pre-shaving, shaving, and after-shave creams for a nationwide billion-dollar close shave!

Americans are also big spenders on diet drinks, diet pills, special low-calorie foods, and fat-reducing machines. People don't need to spend money on these special products to lose weight. Have you seen ads in magazines that tell you how to burn off inches or build bulging biceps in just one month's time? Many people buy these products because they don't feel comfortable about the way they look.

Some beauty products are helpful and healthful. Others can be irritating to the skin, expensive, or unnecessary. It pays to look for natural ways to keep your appearance the way you want it to be — like good food, exercise, time out for relaxation, and plenty of sleep.

Looking Inside Out

Zoom in on your mental snapshot of yourself. Do you think you're taller or smaller, thicker or thinner, lighter or darker than you would like to be? If that snapshot turned into a movie, would you feel comfortable or clumsy watching the way you move around?

How you look, how you feel, and how you move around are all tied up in the private picture you have of yourself. If you feel good about your body, you show it in the way you carry yourself. You share your feelings with others by walking with a special bounce when you're happy or dragging your heels when you're down in the dumps. Does the face you see in the mirror each morning change according to the weather, the coming day's schedule, or the things you're daydreaming about? Your facial expressions and the way you walk are just some of the links between your *outer looks* and your *inner feelings*. There are many more links you will find out about as you read on.

Discover some of the messages you give yourself and the people around you. Explore the body you live in. Find out more about your size, your shape, how you carry your weight, how you move, and the way in which your mind and body work together — or separately.

BODY SNATCHERS

Find a photo of yourself and cut out the head portion. Pick out ten magazine pictures of people with very different body shapes, including one that might fit your "ideal." Try out your head on top of each body in the pictures.

Listening to Your Body

Body Storage Areas

What gives your body its particular shape? You are a mixed bag of bones, muscle, and fat in a combination all your own. The amount of each depends on your age, whether you are a boy or a girl, the family you came from, the way you eat, and your level of physical activity. Bones hold you up, muscles help you move, but what's fat all about?

Your body fat areas act like bank accounts where you can deposit food energy that isn't immediately needed. You withdraw the energy from body fat when you don't have much to eat or are very physically active. When you exercise, your body first uses the available sugars in your bloodstream for energy. Then it uses fat circulating in your bloodstream and stored in *fat cells* all around your body. You change some of this fat to muscle when you get regular exercise. Aerobic exercise is one of the best ways to burn off excess fat.

Where is most of your fat at? Half of it is stored around the major organs like your stomach, heart, intestines and liver, and your muscle groups. The other half is stored directly under the skin. These fat storage areas come in handy cushioning your bones, protecting your organs, and keeping you warm on cold days. But too much fat can add extra work for your heart, lungs, organs, and muscles. When you carry a heavy load of books up a flight of stairs, does your heart beat faster than when you have no load? That's like the extra work the heart of an overweight person must do every day.

HOW CAN BEARS BEAR BARE WINTERS?

Bears who hibernate during the winter go into their hideouts with a thick layer of fat under their skins. As the months pass, their bodies slowly use up this stored fuel energy. What do they look like when they come out again in the spring? _____

One big difference between men and women is the total amount of fat in their bodies. **Men have about 1/8 of their weight in fat; women about 1/5.** This means that a man who weighs 136 pounds has about 17 pounds of fat tucked away, while a woman of the same weight has about 27 pounds. Women have more of the under-the-skin variety stored in the

hips and thighs. Men tend to store fat in the abdominal area.

After your teen years, your body usually increases the amount of fat you have and decreases your lean body weight (non-fat areas). We call this changing balance your *body composition.* Your body composition also reflects the weight of your muscles and the 206 bones which make up your skeleton. If you weigh about 88 pounds, bones take up about 22 pounds and muscles take up about 55 pounds of your total body weight. Your bones are heavier now than they were when you were younger.

Your muscles are heavy parts of you. If you could turn a chunk of fat into a chunk of muscle the same size, it would weigh three times as much. That's why some muscular people who weigh a lot aren't really too heavy for their body size.

POTATO RUN

Run 100 yards. Take your pulse immediately afterwards. Rest for a few minutes. Then run 100 yards again, this time carrying a 10-pound sack of potatoes. Now take your pulse again. Is there any change from your first result?

If flying creatures like birds or bats carried as heavy a skeleton as you do, they'd never get off the ground. Their bones need to be very thin, hollow, and light. On the other hand, the Brontosaurus was able to carry over 30 tons of weight around with him, including some heavy bones and muscles. He did it by remaining in the swamps for most of his life, letting his body half-float as he walked around.

A WHALE OF A TALE

Floating mammals like whales put their body fat to good use. They couldn't float as well without it, or remain warm in the near-freezing Arctic seas where they often live. Whales draw on the food energy stored in their fat when they swim hundreds of miles farther south to bear their young in warm waters. A hundred years ago, whale hunters used this whale fat, called blubber, to make oil for lamps and stoves.

Some of the big 100-ton whales have about 20 tons of blubber, often stored in a layer two feet thick under the paper-thin skin of their body. It keeps them so warm that they have to circulate hot blood through their fins (the only blubberless part of a whale's body) to be cooled off by the ocean water.

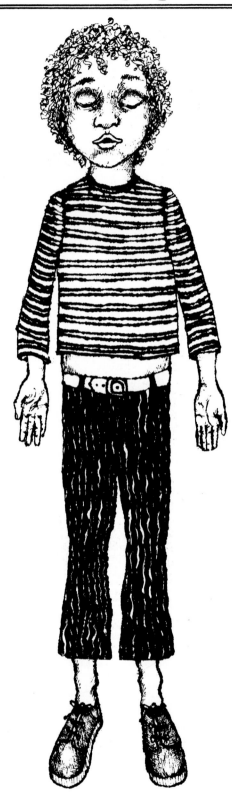

Do your ankles show below your jeans? Does your winter jacket leave your wrists waving in the wind? Maybe you've been growing a lot lately. If you're anywhere between 10 and 15, you may be starting a big growth spurt.

You don't just grow "up," — you grow all over. The different parts of your body are getting bigger at different rates. Your hands and feet grow the fastest, followed by your arms and legs. The slowest change is in the main trunk of your body. So you may feel extra "leggy" for a while before it all evens out.

You used to have quite a head on your shoulders! When you were a baby, your head took up 1/4 of the length of your body. By the time you're 20, it will only take up 1/10 of your length. The organs inside you are also growing at different rates. By age 10, your brain has completed 95 percent of its total growth. But your heart doesn't usually reach its full size until age 20. So you may be a brainy kid already, but you'll be getting heartier in a while.

Your body goes through two fast growing periods in your life. You doubled in height during your first six years of life. Your first year saw the biggest change. From the day you were born until you turned a year old, you may have shot up from about 21 inches to about 30 inches. Suppose you are about 4 feet 8 inches tall, and you kept up that same early rate of growth. You would hit 6 feet 8 inches a year from now!

Your second — and slower — growth spurt usually begins around age 11 for girls and 13 for boys. You'll probably grow 3 to 4 inches every year for a few years. Certain parts of your body will also gradually change, including the width of your shoulders and hips, the length of your arms and legs, the thickness of your chest, and the size of your feet or facial features.

The height you eventually reach when you are about 19 or 20 years old will depend on the kind of body build you inherited from your parents. You also have a say in the process when you eat foods that are rich in the protein, minerals, and vitamins that help you grow and stay healthy.

Reaching Greater Heights

Today, the average height for an American man is about 5 feet 9 inches, while the average height for an American woman is about 5 feet 5 inches. This hasn't always been the case. When the Mayflower arrived in Massachusetts in 1621, the average Pilgrim man was about 5 feet 6 inches tall. What do you think may have caused the change?

We don't know all the reasons, but it is likely that over time, pregnant women and children born in America have had more nutritious food to eat than their parents did. This has helped the younger generations grow to greater heights.

Are there any children in your family who are taller than their parents? Ask your parents if they grew taller than *their* parents of the same sex.

THE TALL AND SHORT OF IT

In East Africa, two neighboring tribes come in very different sizes. The Pygmies are hunters, fishers, and potters who stand at 4 feet 8 inches, at the tallest. The nearby Watusi farmers and cattle herders often grow to a height of 7 feet. If two people from these tribes married and had kids, what do you think their children would look like? _____

World Height Records

Tallest Man:	Height — 8 feet, 11 inches (268 cm) (Robert Wadlow, an American)
Shortest Man:	Height — 26½ inches (66 cm) (Calvin Phillips, an American)
Tallest Woman:	Height — 7 feet, 6½ inches (226 cm) (Wassiliki Calliandji, a Greek)
Shortest Woman:	Height — 23⅕ inches (58 cm) (Pauline Mustarn, a Hollander)

Do You Think You Shrink?

Did you ever dream of suddenly becoming taller or smaller like Alice in Wonderland? Actually, your body could be changing its height at the very time you are dreaming about it at night.

See if it is. Test your shrinkability.

The backbone which holds you upright is made of separate bones called *vertebrae* joined together by elastic *cartilage discs.* These discs act as shock absorbers to cushion the vertebrae when you jump, bend, and twist around. When you stand upright during the day, gravity pulls the bones down and squeezes out the liquid in the discs. When you lie down at night, the liquid has a chance to gather again, making you temporarily taller.

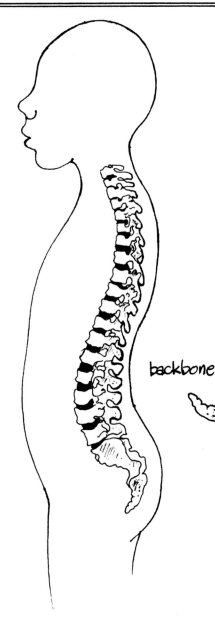

backbone

vertebra

cartilage disc

Astronauts actually grow an inch or two taller while they are in space, because there is no gravity pulling the bones of their spines tightly together.

People sometimes seem to get shorter as they reach their 60's and 70's. They aren't really getting smaller, though. The elastic material between the vertebrae begins to harden as people age. This hardening makes it more difficult for old people to extend their bodies and stand up fully straight, so they end up looking shorter.

Telling Tall Tales

When you were born, you were about 1/3 as tall as you'll grow to be. By the time you were two years old, you reached 1/2 your height. Use your present height to get a general idea of how tall you will eventually be. This will only be a *prediction.* Your real final height will depend on many things, including how well you eat during your teen years.

TEST YOUR SHRINKABILITY

Check out your height as soon as you wake up in the morning. Measure it again later in the day. Did you notice any changes?

Try it out on your parents. Do they shrink more or less than you do?

Predict Your Height

1. Measure your height (in inches or centimeters)

   _____ inches

   or   _____ cm.

2. Add two zeros to your height. _____

3. Divide this number by the number for your age on the chart "Average Percent of Adult Height."

AVERAGE PERCENT OF ADULT HEIGHT

AGE	1	2	3	4	5	6	7	8	9	10	11	12	13	14	15	16	17
GIRLS	45	53	57	62	66	70	74	78	81	84	88	93	97	98	99		
BOYS	42	50	54	58	62	65	69	72	75	78	81	84	87	92	96	98	99

This chart shows what percentage (%) of your predicted adult height you reach at each age. An 11-year-old girl has reached about 88% of her adult height; an 11-year-old boy about 81%. What percentage of your predicted adult height have *you* reached?

4. Your answer tells you about how tall you will be when you are fully grown. You may have already begun a growth spurt which will change the prediction.

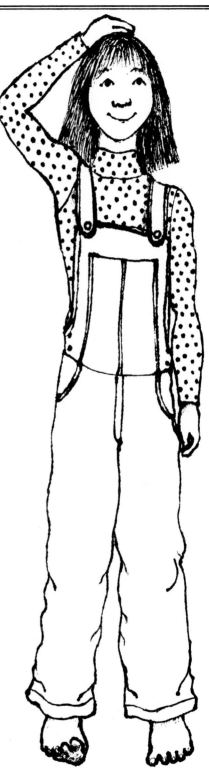

How You Carry Your Weight

The way you walk, stand, sleep, and sit can all have a big impact on how you feel and how easily you move. When you carry your body straight and tall, you are able to breathe deeply and digest your food better. If you slump, you put an extra strain on your muscles and organs. What's more, you don't get to look your friends straight in the eye.

Your body is like a tall building resting on a solid steel frame — your skeleton — which keeps you standing upright. Several millions of years ago, our ancestors crawled around on all fours which made it easy for them to keep their balance as they moved. Today, we humans are the only acrobats in the animal kingdom who have to move around on two stilt-like legs and stay upright as we walk or run.

In order for you to stay in this position day in and day out, you have to rely on the muscles in your back and abdomen to keep your backbone balanced. These muscles must be strong enough to defy the gravity that keeps pulling you down.

If you stand up straight, with shoulders relaxed and stomach and bottom tucked in, **your abdominal and back muscles share the big anti-gravity job of holding you upright.** The rest

of your major muscles can move freely. When you slump forward with your stomach out, your abdominal muscles grow weak and flabby. Your body goes "tilt," and your back muscles have to do an extra support job.

Plenty of adults get backaches from the strain of too many years of slouching. Carrying yourself well now can keep you from having these problems as you get older.

Carrying Your Own Weight

- Stand up or sit tall, as if a puppeteer were holding your body up by a string attached to your head. Keep your shoulders relaxed.

- Bend your knees when you pick up or put down a heavy object.

- Put books or packages in two bags instead of one, so both sides of your body share the burden. Some kids like to carry stuff in a light backpack to distribute the weight evenly over their bodies.

- To strengthen your abdominal muscles, do bent-leg sit-ups. Try to increase the number you do each time.

- To strengthen your back muscles, try the yoga "Bridge" posture.

    1. Lie on your back on a blanket. Bend your knees. Grab your ankles.
    2. Push your back up. Hold for a count of 5 as you breathe in and out.
    3. Slowly lower your back. Straighten your legs. Rest.
    4. Do the exercise twice. If you can hold for a count of 5 after four weeks, try for a count of 10.

Body Signals

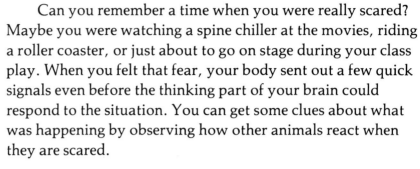

Can you remember a time when you were really scared? Maybe you were watching a spine chiller at the movies, riding a roller coaster, or just about to go on stage during your class play. When you felt that fear, your body sent out a few quick signals even before the thinking part of your brain could respond to the situation. You can get some clues about what was happening by observing how other animals react when they are scared.

That pet alligator you brought home has just escaped from the bathtub and is on the prowl in the backyard! The neighbor's dog and cat stop dead in their tracks. What happens next?

The Cat: His back arches, his hairs stand on end, and he prepares to hiss, scratch, or run.

The Dog: Her body gets poised for action. The pupils of her eyes get bigger and she is ready to snarl, bite, or run.

"SEE YOU LATER, ALLIGATOR!"

Now think back to that movie theater or the minutes before the class play. Did you get goosebumps? Did your eyes open wide or your mouth go dry? Maybe you noticed a change in your heartbeat. Did your heart start racing at about 50 miles per hour while your stomach got tight and queasy?

All these reactions are left-over ways that human beings used to protect themselves when they felt scared or were in danger. When primitive men and women ran into enemies in the forest, they had the choice of either fighting for their lives or quickly running away. At that moment of fear, they needed extra strength in their muscles to help them act quickly. We call

the body changes that helped them in these emergencies the *fight-or-flight response.*

Decoding Your Body Messages

You can learn to decode some of the signals your body sends out when you are angry or scared. Think about those goosebumps. You don't have as much body hair as other mammals like cats, but your hair stands up just the same when you're afraid. Probably thousands of years ago, bristling, fluffed-up hair made scared humans look bigger and fiercer than they really were, so they could ward off a dangerous enemy. Even today we get into some pretty hair-raising experiences.

What about those signals from your heart, stomach, eyes, and mouth? Look at the diagram of the fight-or-flight signals on the next page. **In times of danger, the human body activates the systems that are most needed to get it quickly out of a jam — the heart, lungs, and muscles.** More blood, containing sugar and oxygen, flows to these organs, giving you extra strength and energy. A special messenger hormone called *adrenalin* signals these systems to work at a quicker pace.

During an emergency, less vital functions like digestion have to take a back seat for a while. That is why your saliva flow slows down, leaving you with a dry mouth, your digestive juices don't churn, and you get a tight knot in your stomach. You also begin to sweat as the body's cooling system gets you in gear for heavy action.

We feel the signals of the fight-or-flight response whenever there is a sudden change around us (good or bad) that makes us feel excited or upset. We call these signals of change *stress.* You may not meet up with any man-eaters on your way home from school, but you might sometimes feel the signs of stress when something happens that you don't feel too good about. The stress might show up as a tense feeling in your head, a stomach ache, the jitters, or a night when you can't get to sleep. The happy side of stress — when something new and exciting is about to happen — can also keep you awake at night just thinking happy thoughts.

WAS IT STRESS? YES!

Think of a time when you were very angry or frightened. What did you do? How did you feel? Would a friend have been able to tell what was going on inside you?

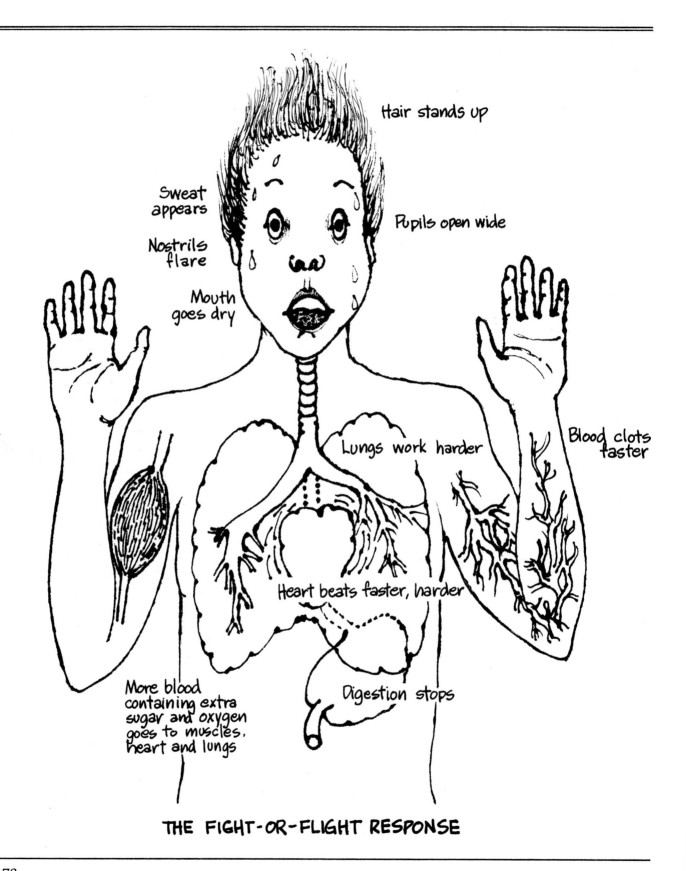

THE FIGHT-OR-FLIGHT RESPONSE

Whenever you feel stress of any sort, the good old fight-or-flight body changes show up. Your muscles get tense and ready to move, while your heart and breathing rates shoot up. The problem is that in today's world we can't just run away or get into a big fight whenever we feel stress. Our bodies are ready to act, but our minds tell us to stay cool.

HOW TO READ MINDS

Where did your little brother hide the package of cookies? Learn how to "read" his mind to find out.

About 50 years ago, a famous magician used to astonish crowds by finding an object that someone in the audience had hidden in the room while the magician was out. He simply led that person by the hand around the room a few times, and — PRESTO! — pointed straight to the hiding place.

How did he do it? First, he checked the person's height, because people often hide things at their arm or shoulder level. The magician kept a close watch on the person's eye movements and sneakily kept his finger on his subject's pulse at the same time. The magician knew that the person would probably avoid looking directly at the hiding place, but his pulse might shoot up instantly and give him away!

WHAT'S THE VERDICT?

A thousand years ago in India and Europe, kings and courts used to decide who was guilty of a crime by making the suspect go through a "trial by ordeal." Body signals were the clues to a person's innocence or guilt. These trials were not very accurate, and innocent people were sometimes burned as witches or executed as criminals. Today, we use more scientific methods and rely on the direct evidence of witnesses.

Here are two real ordeals that were used. Only the names of the characters have been changed to protect the innocent (or guilty). What's *your* verdict?

• An 11-year-old, suspected of poisoning the court jester

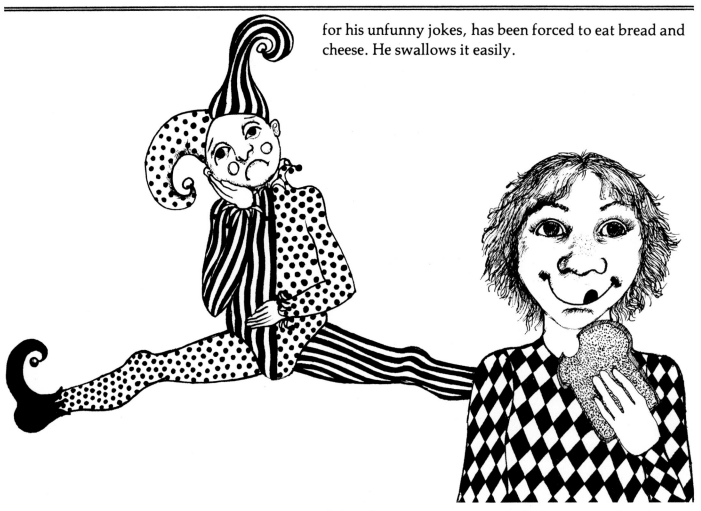

for his unfunny jokes, has been forced to eat bread and cheese. He swallows it easily.

- A handsome stranger, accused of running off with the Maharajah's daughter, has been forced to chew rice. After he spits it out on a leaf, the leaf is still dry.

In modern times, police and courts use mechanical lie detectors to strengthen a lawyer's arguments for a person's guilt or innocence. These machines electronically measure changes in a suspect's heart rate, breathing rate, and amount of sweat given off while he or she is being questioned. Mechanical lie-detectors aren't fool-proof, but they read body signals more accurately than the older ordeals. _____

When Stress Strikes

It's helpful to keep your body in shape to handle stress. If you stay active, your heart and lungs will be ready to handle any extra load that a stressful situation may put on them. **You**

can reduce the tension you feel by getting out and running, going for a long walk, or playing an active game.

Another way to avoid the extra wear and tear on your tense muscles is by **learning new ways to relax, stretch out, breathe deeply,** or **talk out your feelings.** Next time you feel stress, watch for changes in your body. Listen to your heart and breathing rates and pay attention to signals from your mouth, skin, and stomach. Maybe when you're in a fight with a friend you can both quit early and check each other's body changes!

Some adults who live with too much stress don't find ways of releasing it. Many of them end up with headaches, backaches, or stomach trouble. Their fight-or-flight response puts them in high gear too often. What do they do about it? **People often try to relieve stress by taking pills, smoking, overeating, or drinking.** These are expensive and harmful escapes. Americans spend over $200 million each year on *tranquilizers,* calming drugs which are the most commonly prescribed pills in America today. They also spend millions of dollars on pills to relieve aches and pains that are symptoms of stress.

Other people drink, smoke, or eat their blues away. In 1978, Americans spent over $20 billion on alcoholic beverages, or $100 for every man, woman, and child. Ten million people in this country are alcoholics who need to have several drinks just to get through the day. Some people get hooked on cigarettes in order to relax, others reach for a snack and get into the habit of overeating.

People who exercise regularly and build relaxation into their lives have less need for these artificial stress relievers. The pages which follow offer some simple ways to reduce tension.

Get to know your body signals better. As you begin to understand what your body is saying when you are happy, angry, excited, or afraid, you can learn new ways to handle some of the crazy events of life with greater ease.

ADS THAT MENTION TENSION
How many advertised products can you think of that claim to relieve stress of tension headaches, backaches, stomach-aches, or lack of sleep (insomnia)?

You can have a two-way conversation with your body to relax it whenever you get a tight feeling in your neck, stomach, shoulders, or all over. Relaxing can help you in those fight-or-flight situations, when you want to loosen tense muscles and slow down your breathing and heartbeat. It can keep you alert and give you an extra dose of energy when you are working hard. Here are a few relaxercisers that may come in handy.

The big key to relaxing is to concentrate on your *insides*, not your *outsides.* To get uptight muscles un-tight, get better acquainted with those muscles. This first exercise can help you. It is based on the scientific fact that after you tighten up a muscle by squeezing it hard, it is easier to relax it, to let it go completely limp. As all your muscles relax one by one, your whole body feels less tense.

The Sponge

Ask a friend or a relative to read these instructions out to you as you try doing the Sponge the first time. Then switch places, and let the other person try it.

Lie on your back on a flat surface. Close your eyes. Picture yourself a sponge lying in a puddle on a sunny day. Breathe slowly and deeply.

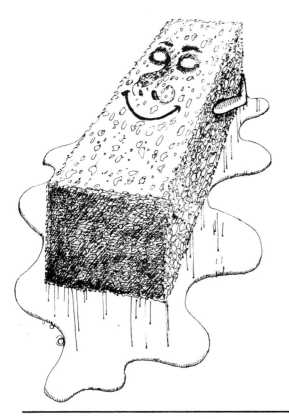

1. *Start by thinking about your right foot.*
   Curl the toes. Tighten the muscles. Point the right foot out, then up, then let it go loose.

2. *Do the same with your left foot.*
   Curl the toes. Tighten the muscles. Point your left foot out, up, and let it go loose.

3. *Feel the muscles in your right leg.*
   Tighten your right calf. Tighten your right thigh. Pull up your knee. Let your leg go down straight again. Relax your whole right leg.

4. *Feel the muscles in your left leg.*
   Tighten your left calf. Tighten your left thigh. Pull up your knee. Let your leg go down straight again. Relax your whole left leg.

5. *Feel the lower part of your body going limp. Now turn*

your mind to the trunk of your body.
Tighten your bottom, hold, and let go. Pull your stomach in as far as you can, hold, and let go. Arch your spine, pushing your chest out, and let go. Shrug your shoulders, then relax.

6. *Now get in touch with your hands and arms beginning with your right side.*
Stretch out the fingers on your right hand. Make a fist. Let your right hand go. Tighten the muscles in your right forearm. Then let them go.

7. *Left side.*
Stretch out the fingers on your left hand. Make a fist. Let your left hand go. Tighten the muscles in your left forearm. Then let them go.

8. *Now feel the muscles of your face.*
Smile, Purse your lips (as if you were going to kiss someone). Frown. Squeeze your eyes tightly shut and move your eyeballs in two complete circles. Then relax them. Yawn slowly.

Your whole body should feel relaxed. Let yourself float like a sponge that has soaked up water. Breathe in and out slowly four times. Feel your heartbeat. Do you notice any difference between now and the times when you are active?

Take a deep breath and hold it as you raise your arms slowly over your head. Stretch like a cat. Breathe out. Shake loose. Stand up slowly. Re-charge your energy as you head back to work or play.

Untying the Knots

This is a relaxerciser for the skeletal muscles. It was a favorite of the ancient Chinese Kung Fu warriors who were about to undergo vigorous training for combat.

1. Stand tall with your shoulders relaxed. Let your arms and hands hang loosely at your sides.

2. Shake both arms and hands as if you were shaking off drops of water after taking a swim.

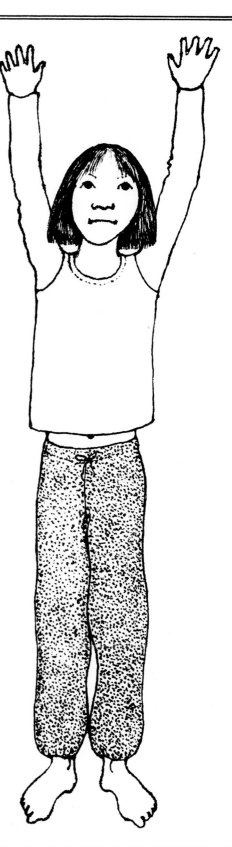

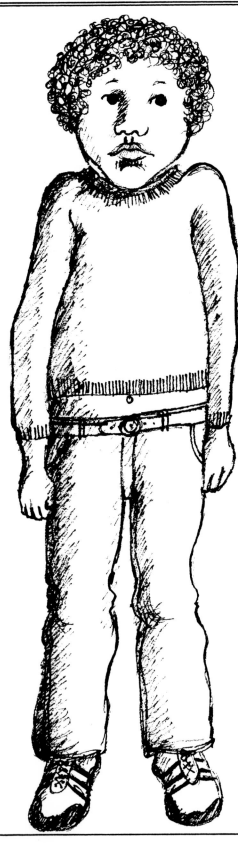

3. Lift your right leg and shake it gently, then your left leg.

4. Relax your neck muscles by letting your head drop forward as far as possible.

5. Slowly revolve your head from right to left for two full turns, then reverse direction for two turns.

6. Bring your arms up in front of you, with palms facing the floor, breathing in.

7. Continue moving your arms upward until you are stretching up to the ceiling, lifting yourself up onto the balls of your feet.

8. Hold for a count of five, then breathe out as you slowly bring your arms down to your sides and your heels back to the floor.

9. Stand completely still. Feel your muscles relax.

Try this two times.

For times when there is no mat or floor space nearby, try these quickies:

Neck Rolls: Roll your neck around slowly from right to left, and then reverse. Do this two or three times.

I Don't Know: You *do* know it. Just shrug your shoulders a few times. It's a handy relaxerciser for those times when you don't know the right answer in class!

A Breath of Fresh Air

Take a pause that refreshes in the middle of your busy day. Deep breathing can bring you a feeling of calm wherever you are.

Try it first lying down on a mat or rug to feel the way your body draws in air when you are asleep. Lie on your back, with one hand resting lightly on your abdomen. Inhale slowly through your nose. Feel your abdomen move outward as if a balloon were filling up inside you. Your chest should hardly move at all. Hold this position for a few seconds, then exhale

slowly through your nose or mouth, pulling in your stomach muscles slightly as you do.

After a practice try, set up a slow and steady rhythm for yourself by counting. You might try counting slowly to four as you breathe in, again to four as you hold, and to eight as you slowly breathe out all the air inside. But everyone has his or her own rhythm, and you may find that a different count suits you better.

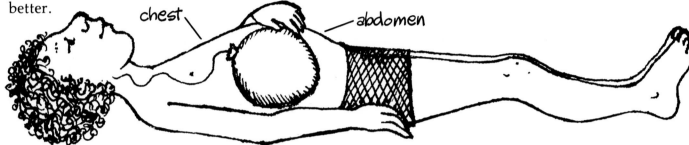

chest   abdomen

Some people who have practiced yoga deep breathing for many years can reduce the amount of oxygen their bodies need and take more air into their bodies with each deep breath. Yogis in India and religious monks in Japan have been known to get enough air in a single breath to last them for several minutes.

IN - 2 - 3 - 4

HOLD - 2 - 3 - 4

OUT - 2 - 3 - 4 - 5 - 6 - 7 - 8

Deep breathing helps you strengthen the rib muscles and diaphragm that you use actively when you do aerobic exercise. Practice deep breathing any time, anywhere, sitting or lying down.

WHODUNIT? HOUDINI!

Did you ever get that boxed-in feeling? The great magician, Houdini, practiced special breathing techniques for years to help him get out of boxes, coffins, trunks, paper bags sealed with wax, and even a preserved giant squid!

One of his most famous acts was the Chinese Water torture escape, first attempted in public in 1913. He was lowered, head first, with his feet chained together, into a large wood and glass cabinet filled with water. A curtain was drawn. The audience waited breathlessly for him to get out. People began to whisper and grow restless. A few minutes later, when hope was almost lost, out walked Houdini, smiling and dripping wet.

What was the secret to his daring escape? Part of it was special breathing techniques. Another part was his remarkable degree of physical fitness. He had to be flexible enough to worm his way out of straight-jackets and strong enough to untie heavy cords and lift off chains. The public didn't know that another "key" to Houdini's success was his training as a locksmith. Duplicate keys, hidden scissors, nail clippers, and dummy nails all played a role in Houdini's many years of mystery escapes. For the Chinese Water Torture Cell stunt, a special slide-out box also helped. _____

Meditation — Putting Your Mind at Rest

Did you ever stare at a fire, a candle, or a cloud until your mind felt peaceful and relaxed? What you did was a kind of **meditation — the ancient Asian art of relaxing by getting the mind very quiet and still.** Over 1 million people around the world have turned to meditation as one way of reducing the tensions in their lives.

There are many ways to meditate. Most people first find a quiet place with no distractions. That could be a lonely spot in a park or the woods, a corner of an empty room, or a place of worship like a temple, church, synagogue, or mosque. Then people who meditate focus on a sound or word inside their heads which they repeat over and over. This helps them empty their heads of all thoughts. When ideas or images come to mind, they simply let these thoughts pass on. They make sure to sit in a comfortable position.

Many people meditate more than once a day. They may take a twenty-minute break before breakfast, while sitting in a train or a bus, instead of a coffee break at work, or in the evenings after work. Meditation gives these people extra energy and concentration. Some people who meditate find they sleep longer and more deeply. Others find they are more aware of what is going on around them — and inside them. When you meditate, you listen to your body more carefully.

What happens inside the body of a person who is meditating? We don't know all the facts, but scientists have observed certain changes:

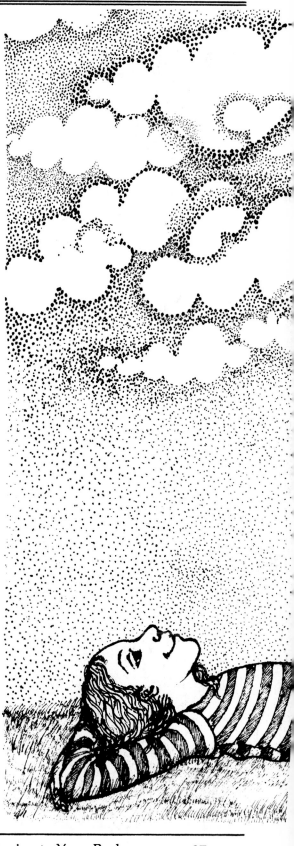

- Your body uses less oxygen (as little as you need after 4 to 5 hours of sleep).

- Your heart rate, breathing rate, and blood pressure go down.

- Your brain makes more *alpha waves* (signs of deep relaxation).

These changes are the opposite of the fight-or-flight response. In fact, meditation is often called the *"relaxation response."*

Some doctors encourage their patients with high blood pressure or heart disease to meditate every day. There are signs that meditation can help these patients reduce the ill effects of these diseases. For whatever reasons people choose to meditate, they find it a natural way to feel calmer in our fast-paced world.

Relaxercisers, deep breathing, and meditation are just some of the ways people can help themselves stay healthy. Physical activity can also help your body stay fit. How does the food you eat affect the way you look and feel? What does it say about you? Read on for the inside story of food and you.

FOOD CHOICES

Take a Taste Test

Do you know why you eat what you do? Here is a chance to find out more about it. Number a piece of paper from 1 to 8 and see if you agree with these statements. Some have no right or wrong answers. They depend on what *you* do or think.

1. TERMITES AND OTHER INSECTS ARE GOOD FOOD.

2. THE MORE I PAY FOR FOOD, THE BETTER IT IS FOR ME.

3. I EAT AT HOME MORE OFTEN THAN I EAT IN RESTAURANTS.

4. SOMETIMES WHEN I'M REALLY HUNGRY, I'LL EAT FOOD I USUALLY WOULDN'T TOUCH.

5. MEAT IS THE MOST IMPORTANT PROTEIN FOOD FOR PEOPLE ALL OVER THE WORLD.

6. MILK IS A GOOD FOOD FOR EVERYONE.

7. MY RELIGION SOMETIMES INFLUENCES THE FOOD I EAT.

8. WHEN MY GRANDPARENTS OR GREATGRANDPARENTS CAME TO THIS COUNTRY, THE FIRST THING THEY CHANGED WAS THEIR FOOD.

Answers

1. **Termites and other insects are good food.**
   Yes, they are. Fresh and fried termites are eaten and enjoyed by many people in Asia and Africa. The termites there are larger and more numerous than our local ones. Termites are half *protein.* They are just one of the possible nutritious insect foods that we usually avoid in our culture.

2. **The more I pay for food, the better it is for me.**
   No. The high cost of food you buy may be caused by the number of changes it goes through before it reaches you. Many expensive ready-to-eat foods have added ingredients like sugar, salt, and preservatives, and they come in fancy packages. You are paying for the *processing* that changed those foods. You are also paying for the trucks that brought them to you and the advertising and packaging that got you to buy them, not for the nutrients they contain.

3. **I eat at home more often than I eat in restaurants.**
   If you eat at home more often, you are in the company of most Americans who eat two out of three meals at home. But predictions are that by the 1980's, we will be eating half of our meals in restaurants.

4. **Sometimes when I'm really hungry, I'll eat food I usually wouldn't touch.** There may have been times in your life when you had to eat new foods because your old choices weren't available. Maybe it was when you ate over at a friend's house. Emergencies have often forced people to eat new foods in order to survive. When they were starving during World War II, the Dutch ate tulip bulbs, and the Russians ate cats, dogs, and rats.

5. **Meat is the most important protein food for people all over the world.** No. Meat is a luxury in many countries. It is a good source of protein, but it is expensive. A lot of land is required to grow the grain plants such as wheat and corn that are used to feed cattle. That same land could feed many more people if they ate the grains instead of meat. Many Asians and South Americans depend on plant food combinations like rice and beans as their main source of protein. How many times a week does your family eat

meat? Do you ever eat meals with plant food combinations as the main course?

6. **Milk is a good food for everyone.**
No. Although milk is a great food for most infants and growing children, it is not so good for some adults. Milk contains a sugar called lactose. Many adults of African and Asian backgrounds don't have enough of the *enzyme* in their bodies that they need to digest this sugar. So when they drink more than a glass of milk, they get cramps and gas.

7. **My religion sometimes influences the food I eat.**
If you are an Orthodox Jew or a Moslem, your religion forbids you to eat pork. Many religions forbid or restrict the use of certain foods. There are some days of the year when Catholics may not eat meat. Jews eat matzo instead of bread during Passover. Food can also be a symbol in religious rituals. Christians use bread and wine in the Communion service, and Jews use bitter herbs and a lamb bone as part of the Passover Seder.

8. **When my grandparents or great-grandparents came to this country, the first thing they changed was their food.**
No. If your grandparents or great-grandparents were like most American immigrants, their food habits were probably the last thing they changed. Most new immigrants first changed the way they dressed and tried to learn the new language. Food habits were slow to change, because eating was done at home, in private. How many foods from your grandparents' or great-grandparents' countries do you still eat?

Food Talks

FOOD EXPRESSIONS

How corny can you get?

Doesn't know beans.

A piece of cake.

He's a ham.

You're chicken.

That's a lot of bologna.

The apple of your eye.

You may not realize it, but **food creeps into your conversation all the time,** and sometimes when you least expect it. You don't believe it? Well, chew on it for a while, and you soon may.

How do you feel when your Aunt Henrietta lands a big whopping kiss on her "sweetie-pie" or offers her "honey dear" a chewy box of chocolates? Do you lap it up? Or can't you stomach it when she talks that way? It's amazing how often people use sweet talk to show they care for someone. They also use food expressions to show whether they're talking about a serious "meaty" subject, or about something that isn't worth "peanuts."

You'll find food words constantly on the tip of your tongue. To get a better idea of how food "talks," try these activities:

MAKE A LIST OF COMMON EXPRESSIONS USING FOOD

Act them out, one at a time, with a group of your classmates. The person who guesses right gets to act out the next food expression.

NOW MAKE UP A FEW NEW SAYINGS OF YOUR OWN

Decide which foods to use and what you want them to mean. Use your new food expressions with your friends and family for a while. Did anyone else start using your food sayings? Did you use theirs?

Food Clues

People have always had many different reasons for choosing their food. In ancient Rome, banquet guests were served meats according to their Zodiac signs. The Gemini (twins) would get paired kidneys for their main course. It might be easy to have a Pisces (fish) or a Cancer (crab) to dinner, but what if you had a Leo (lion) at your table? And the Chinese used to serve up a dish of bats for those who couldn't see too well or were hard of hearing.

Let's take a look at the meal *you* had for dinner last night. What does it say about you? Why do you think that meal made it to your table? Is it because your family loves the **taste** of Mom's spaghetti sauce? Or is it because drumsticks were **on sale**? Were chili leftovers from the freezer all you had **time** for? **The food you eat can give lots of clues about who you are, where you live, how active your day is, and how much you know about good nutrition.**

Food can also tell time. Though a hamburger strapped to your wrist may not be quite as accurate as a watch, **food can tell something about what time of year it is or what historic period you are living in.** For example, a frozen yogurt cone may tell you it's summertime in the U.S.A. in the 1980's. Food remembers (and may tell) who your grandparents were, where you have traveled, and what your religion and traditions are.

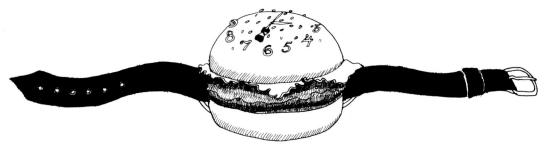

So food talks, you say? It spills the beans. Take another look at last night's dinner. How would that meal change if your favorite, but toothless, Great-aunt Gertrude were coming to dinner? Or if it were your birthday? What if it were harvest time in your garden? What would you eat on the fifth snowed-in day after the Great Boston Blizzard of 1978?

Is there pineapple in your iced tea or squid in your spaghetti? Are there termites on your toast? You can get clues from what's *not* on your plate too.

Pick Your Favorites

Try this activity to get a start on finding out why you choose the foods you do.

Number a piece of paper from 1 to 10. Then make a list of your ten favorite foods. You can include anything — your favorite dinner, snacks, fruits and vegetables, lunches, or your own inventions.

When you finish your list, mark seven columns next to it to make a chart like the one below.

FOOD	TOP 3 FAVORITES	SEASON	RESTAURANT	GRAND-PARENTS' COUNTRIES	SPECIAL OCCASIONS	FROM FOREIGN COUNTRY	NEW
1. lasagna	*	A	✓			✓	✓
2. peach							
3. taco							
4. yogurt							

1. In the first column put a * next to the three foods you like best. If you asked your parents their three favorite foods, do you think they'd pick the same three as yours?

2. In the second column mark the season of the year you eat those ten favorites. Write "S" for summer, "F" for fall, "Sp" for spring, "W" for winter, and "A" for foods for all seasons.

3. Check (✓) the third column for those foods that you eat only in restaurants.

4. Check (✓) the fourth column next to the foods that come from the countries where your grandparents or great-grandparents lived before they landed in America.

5. Check (✓) the fifth column for the foods you eat mostly on special occasions like birthdays or Thanksgiving or the last day of school.

6. Check (✓) the sixth column for any food that comes from a foreign country (like egg roll or lasagna).

7. Check (✓) the seventh column for any new favorite that you wouldn't have listed two years ago.

    What did you find out about your food choices from your list?

    - Are your favorites part of a meal or a snack? Are they summer fruits, sweet desserts, or home-cooked specialties from other countries? Are they frozen, fresh, or canned? What are some of the similar things about your favorite foods?

    - What things affect your choices more than others?

    - Compare your favorites with those of other kids in your class. What are their reasons for choosing their favorite foods?

A Small Taste of History

You may be surprised to find out how much our American food supply and eating habits have changed in the past 70 or even 20 years.

Here are a few sample changes:

FOOD CONSUMPTION PER PERSON PER YEAR

	1910	1976
Apples (fresh)	54 pounds	15 pounds
Fruit (fresh)	52 pounds	38 pounds
Beef	62 pounds	100 pounds

	1926	1976
Tuna (canned)	less than ½ pound	3 pounds

	1940	1976
Vegetables (frozen)	½ pound	10 pounds

	1960	1976
Soft drinks	200 8-ounce servings	493 8-ounce servings
Potatoes	80 pounds	48 pounds

As you can see from the table above, we don't eat as many fresh apples, other fresh fruits, or potatoes as we used to. **New ways of processing and selling food have caused some of these changes.** Today we eat many more frozen vegetables and fruits. Your grandparents probably didn't have as many freeze-dried or frozen foods available to them as you do today.

Five-and-a-half times as many potatoes were frozen in 1976 as in 1960. French fries are the reason. Most frozen potatoes go the french fry route in fast food restaurants. There probably weren't even any fast food restaurants around in your grandparents' childhood.

The availability of fresh foods has also changed a great deal in the past 150 years. In 1835, fresh strawberries were available in northern U.S. cities only one month a year. By 1865, you could find strawberries during four months of the year. Today, fresh strawberries are available year-round if you don't mind paying the price of bringing them from California and Mexico in the winter.

Many fresh fruits and vegetables are available more months a year, thanks to new plant varieties and to modern transportation by refrigerated trucks and trains. Which of your favorite fruits and vegetables can you get fresh only at certain times of the year? Look at the tables on this page to see.

FRESH FRUITS AND VEGETABLES AVAILABLE YEAR ROUND IN THE U.S.

apples, bananas, beans, beets, broccoli, cabbage, carrots, celery, cucumbers, grapefruit, grapes, lettuce, onions, oranges, pears, pineapples, potatoes, radishes, strawberries, tomatoes.

FRESH FRUITS AVAILABLE IN THE U.S. PART OF THE YEAR

	MAR	APR	MAY	JUNE	JULY	AUG	SEPT	OCT	NOV	DEC
Apricots			•	•	•	•				
Blueberries			•	•	•	•	•			
Cantaloupe	•	•	•	•	•	•	•	•	•	
Sweet cherries			•	•	•	•				
Cranberries							•	•	•	•
Peaches			•	•	•	•	•	•		
Plums				•	•	•	•	•		
Pomegranates						•	•	•	•	•
Watermelon	•	•	•	•	•	•	•			

Seventy or more different kinds of fresh fruits and vegetables may be in the market at the same time. Even when snow covers the frozen ground, you can buy 50 different fruits and vegetables. This means that your food has to travel long distances to reach you.

U.S. chickens and their eggs travel an average of 1,200 miles from farm to table. Fresh fruits and vegetables may have to be trucked 2,000 miles. For New England, those distances are often greater. Winter supplies of spinach come from Texas, tomatoes and cucumbers from Mexico, and beans from Florida. Four out of five lettuce heads eaten in New England have traveled 3,000 miles from California. In fact, it takes three times as much energy to get a California lettuce leaf to its Boston salad bowl as it takes to grow it. **The biggest ingredient in getting much of our food to our table is the diesel fuel it takes to truck it around.** And fuel is getting more costly and less available.

Why does our food have to travel such long distances? What happened to all the local farms? In Massachusetts between 1930 and 1974, the number of farms decreased from almost 26,000 to 5,000. A decrease in the number of farms and acreage has taken place in many other states as well. Today's

larger farms use great amounts of energy for fertilizers and machinery. They use new plant varieties that produce larger crop yields. But we are paving over much of our fertile and valuable crop lands to put in buildings and parking lots. So we are no longer able to grow as many food crops locally.

Your grandparents may have grown up or worked on a farm, or at least had one nearby where they bought their fresh fruits, vegetables, eggs, and milk. You may be saving some energy with a summer backyard vegetable garden if you belong to one of the 32 million American families that raised their own fruits and vegetables in 1977. Those vegetables and fruits don't have to travel so far to your table. But it's still a good bet that you and your family get most of your food year-round from the local supermarket, and that food *is* well-traveled.

CHICK' N' EGG FARM

Food Choices

Three Generation Questionnaire

To find out first-hand how our food supply and eating habits have changed over the years, try these questions on your family and friends. First interview yourself to check out your present eating habits. Then interview one of your parents and, finally, a grandparent, or a neighbor or friend who's in the same generation as your grandparents are or would be. When you finish, you can **compare the way you eat now to the way your parents and grandparents ate when they were your age.**

1. What foods did you and your family eat when you were a child that you don't eat as much of now? How did your *ethnic background* influence the foods you ate? What is that background?

2. Where did you get your food? (Your answer should be specific: supermarket, farmer's market, garden, farm, milkman, etc.)

3. Who prepared your meals? How much time did the cook spend on meal preparation?

4. How were your mealtimes as a child different from the way they are for most children today?

5. What days of the week or year did you eat special meals when you were a child?

6. Did you eat any special home-remedy foods when you were sick? What were they?

7. What foods do you like or dislike because they remind you of places, things, or people of the past?

8. Which foods do you eat now that seemed strange or unappetizing when they were first introduced to you?

9. What major changes in food processing have occurred since you were a child? What kinds of gadgets or new foods have become available?

10. What changes in food since your childhood do you think are improvements? What changes do you regret?

Food Choice Boxes

How do your daily activities affect your food choices?

- Who cooks the meals in your family? Does he or she work outside the home full-time?

- How are your weekday dinners different from weekend dinners?

- Do you or your parents ever have to be somewhere right after dinner? How does that change what you have for dinner?

- How much time do you have for lunch in school? How are your lunches there different from your lunches at home?

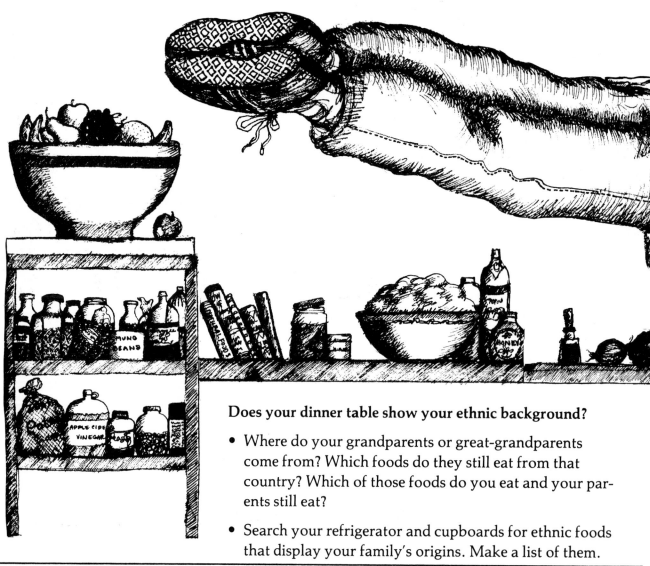

Does your dinner table show your ethnic background?

- Where do your grandparents or great-grandparents come from? Which foods do they still eat from that country? Which of those foods do you eat and your parents still eat?

- Search your refrigerator and cupboards for ethnic foods that display your family's origins. Make a list of them.

How do your senses of sight, taste, smell, touch, and temperature affect your food choices? Look at your favorite meal.

- What colors do you find?

- What kinds of tastes are there: sweet, sour, salty, or bitter?

- Which smells do you like best? Describe them.

- What crunchy, chewy, or soft foods do you like?

- Do you like cold foods? Do you prefer your soup steaming hot or lukewarm?

Are there foods that are special family traditions in your house?

- Do they make you think of special celebrations?

- Are there foods that are forbidden in your family, like pork, lobster, beef, or termites?

How would a food story sound from a food's point of view?

Listen to this interview with a Fenway Frank:

"THIS KID IS A RED SOX FAN AND HE NEEDS ONE HAND FREE FOR A FLY BALL. THAT'S WHY I COME IN HANDY. YOU KNOW IT'S HARD TO EAT LASAGNA IN THE BLEACHERS. HE DOESN'T GET A BIG ALLOWANCE AND I DON'T COST MUCH. HE NEEDS TO EAT A LOT BECAUSE HE'S GROWING. WHAT TIME OF YEAR IS IT? SUMMER, OF COURSE, AND ....."

WRITE YOUR OWN SHORT STORY OR INTERVIEW
FROM THE MEAL'S POINT OF VIEW.
 CHOOSE A MEAL AND WRITE WHAT IT WOULD
TELL ABOUT YOU — WHO YOU ARE, WHERE YOU
ARE, THE TIME OF YEAR, WHO YOUR GRAND-
PARENTS ARE, ETC.

Show and Sell

HAVE TV ADS GOTTEN THROUGH TO YOU?

Try completing these food product jingles:

_____ - it's mostly nuts.

_____ adds life!

You deserve a break today, so get out and get away to _____.

____ are, mm, mm, good.

Oh-oh, _____.

_____ is a natural.

Have you ever bought a food you saw advertised on television? By the time most kids graduate from high school they have spent an average of 15,000 hours watching TV and 11,000 hours in school. All that TV watching includes 10,000 commercials a year just about food.

Do all those commercials have an effect on you? The advertisers spend a lot of money to make sure they do. Some advertisers spend $125,000 for a one-minute commercial! And they may not have your best nutritional interests in mind when they plan that minute. When was the last time you saw a TV commercial for an apple or a carrot?

More than half the foods advertised to kids on TV are highly sugared and highly processed, ready-to-eat snack foods like cakes, cookies, candies and sweetened cereals. In 1976, the average American ate almost 17 pounds of candy. And some heavily advertised breakfast cereals have as much sugar in each serving as a candy bar.

Most dentists agree that *refined sugar* which is found in great amounts in cookies, candies, soft drinks, and pre-sweetened breakfast cereals is a major cause of tooth decay. Kids in the Boston area alone form 4,000 new cavities a day. **Remember, the advertisers' business is selling products, not nutrition.**

How do those advertisers manage to convince you that you can't do without their product? Do they tell you that "Wonder Junk"

- makes you more popular?
- gives you the energy to leap tall fire hydrants at a single bound?
- comes with a free, life-size rubber snake that will make you the hit of your class?

Advertisements try to convince you that you *need* the product they are selling.

Keeping a Count on Commercials

Take a close look at TV commercials.

Watch the TV ads during an hour of Saturday morning television time.

Make a chart like the one below to keep track of the information you collect:

1. Count the number of ads.

2. How many advertise food? Keep track of the kinds and numbers of foods advertised. How many commercials are for snack foods, cereals, or candies? How many promote fresh fruits, vegetables, fish, or milk products?

3. What information is given about each product? How does that help you to decide whether to buy it or not?

4. What special effects are used in making the commercials? (Fancy lighting, sound effects, different camera angles, small print, backgrounds, etc.)

5. Does the commercial make you want to buy the product?

Now watch an hour of evening prime-time TV between 7:30 and 9:30 p.m., and compare the ads to the kinds you saw on Saturday morning. Keep the same kind of chart for the evening shows so you can compare all the details.

Day _____ Time _____ Channel _____

Name of product advertised	Kind of product Food Other		Kind of food	Information they give you about the product	Ways they convince you to buy it	Special effects	Does the commercial make you want to buy it?
Loopo Cereal	x		cereal	It's chocolate cereal. It's fun to eat. It'll give you quick energy	Send away Loopo shirt offer.	Background music, Giggling, Kids eating the cereal	no

Restaurant Roots

One of the reasons you have so many food choices is because our country is made up of people from all over the world. People from a particular country who share language and customs are said to have the same ethnic background. **Choice of food is one of the signs of ethnic differences.**

For 300 years, waves of immigrants to America have brought us special dishes from their old countries. Italian immigrants brought us mozarella cheese and pasta specialties like ravioli and lasagna. Mexicans have introduced us to tacos and hot chili dishes. A hundred years ago, German settlers arrived with sausages and sauerkraut, and a curious chopped beefsteak dish named after the city of Hamburg, Germany. This "hamburger" was introduced at the St. Louis World's Fair in 1909 and became a hit overnight! We owe many popular American foods to groups of settlers who adapted their old recipes to the local crops, climate, and customs of our country. They have helped make food in this country the most varied in the world.

When settlers first arrived, they usually kept their old ways of eating within their family and community. Until the middle of the 1800's, most American immigrants were farmers and settled in small towns all over the country. After about 1870, many newcomers flocked to neighborhoods in big cities where fellow countrymen were already living.

The immigrants in cities often set up eating places where they could eat familiar foods and speak their own language. These restaurants became places where friends could meet to talk about their new lives in a strange country. Gradually more and bigger restaurants opened up as ethnic foods became more popular with the general public. As immigrants' children and grandchildren moved to new places, ethnic restaurants often followed them.

People from different backgrounds now live in all parts of our country. You couldn't find too many pizza places in small American towns 25 years ago. Today, you would have to look

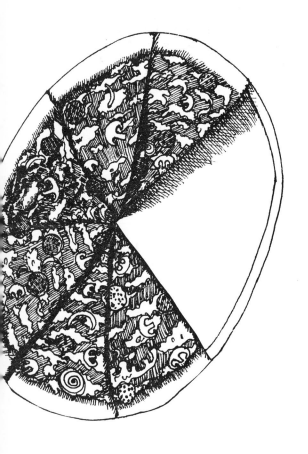

pretty hard to find a town without one. Many regions have special dishes handed down from the settlers who arrived there. Are there special ethnic foods and festivals in your part of the country?

Ethnic foods give us a glimpse of the enormous variety of foods in the world. When you try Hungarian goulash or Chinese sweet and sour chicken, you sample a bit of life from a different country. If you eat some of the foods that your ancestors used to eat, you take a time machine trip back to your family's past.

LET YOUR FINGERS DO THE EATING

Check the restaurants section of the yellow pages in your area. How many kinds of ethnic restaurants do you find? Which national foods seem to be the most popular? Do you know if many people of that background live in your town or city?

Each country has developed its own special ways of preparing everyday foods or special holiday dishes. Homemade soups, breads, desserts, and beverages all use locally available ingredients, but the results are amazingly different. Let's say you took a basic grain — like wheat — and ground it into flour, pounded it, kneaded it, fried or baked it. You might end up with a golden loaf of bread, a puffy fritter, a twisted pretzel, or a flat, thin pancake, depending on which ethnic cooking style you used.

Each country has used one of the important grain foods of the world to develop delicious dishes. In cold climates like Scotland, people preferred to cook with the rye or oats that grew there. In parts of China and India where rice is commonly grown, that became the most common food in the diet. In the Americas, corn was the native crop used in all early American cooking.

An International House of Pancakes

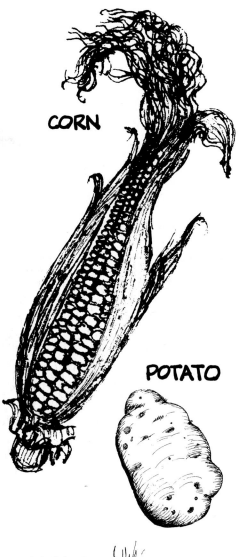

CORN

POTATO

WHEAT

OATS

Think about the simple pancake. Does that seem like a typical American dish? It is, but in different shapes with a few different ingredients, it is really a dish of the world. Use your imagination. Come with us on a trip around the world with the pancake as your guide.

Mexico: *Tortillas* are flatcakes made from corn or maize, the biggest crop in all the Americas. If you wrap a tortilla around beans or meat, grated cheese, and salad, you have a *taco.* If you break it into small pieces and fry them in corn oil, you have fritos or corn chips.

North America — New England: The Indians taught the early English settlers how to make *johnnycakes* out of corn meal. Travelers used to pack these flat round pancakes in their saddle bags to eat as they journeyed. Traveling preachers and judges would carry them from town to town. What began as a "journeycake" eventually became known as a "johnnycake."

North America — The South: Similar cornmeal cakes, called *hush puppies,* were deep fried until they puffed into fritters. Sometimes hunters would quiet their yelping, hungry hounds by tossing them a pancake and crying, "Hush, puppy!"

Eastern Europe: *Potato latkes* are pancakes made of grated potatoes and eggs. They are a traditional favorite during the Jewish holiday of Hanukkah.

Ireland: *Boxty-on-the-pan* is the Irish version of the potato pancake.

Scotland: Scottish oatcakes called *bannocks* are usually served with cheese or marmalade. Scottish soldiers used to carry oatmeal with them wherever they went and sometimes lived for days on oatcakes alone.

India: *Chapatis* are whole wheat flat breads cooked by Indian families. They are often used instead of forks for scooping up food. Sometimes secret messages are sent from village to village by folded chapatis. The special way they are folded tells the secret date or event.

France: Very thin pancakes called *crepes* are a favorite food in France. Sometimes they are sold on the street for snacks. They

can be eaten plain, sprinkled with sugar or jam, or filled with vegetables, fish, or cheese.

Russia: Thin pancakes similar to crepes are called *blinis* or *blintzes* in Russia and Eastern Europe. Some favorite fillings are farmer's cheese and potatoes.

THE GREAT PANCAKE RACE

Did you ever see a bunch of people running down the streets flipping pancakes as they went? Kids in Olney, England and Liberal, Kansas see that kind of pancake race each spring.

Over 500 years ago, a housewife in Olney was late getting to church. It was Shrove Tuesday, the day before the beginning of Lent, a time of fasting for Christians. Instead of heading off for church, she was busy making pancakes to use up all the fats in her house which were forbidden during Lent.

When she heard the churchbells ring, she dashed out of the house. She was in such a rush that she kept her apron and scarf on, and took her pancake griddle with her!

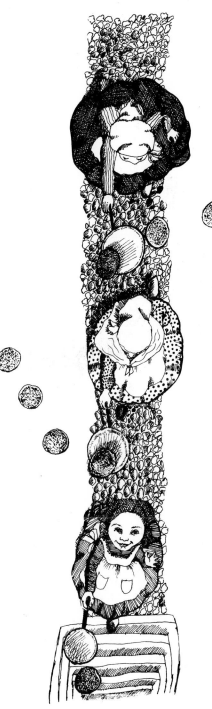

     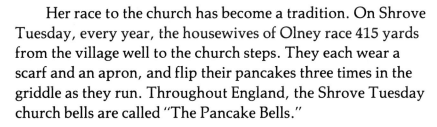

Her race to the church has become a tradition. On Shrove Tuesday, every year, the housewives of Olney race 415 yards from the village well to the church steps. They each wear a scarf and an apron, and flip their pancakes three times in the griddle as they run. Throughout England, the Shrove Tuesday church bells are called "The Pancake Bells."

Thirty years ago, some people in the town of Liberal, Kansas, saw a photo of the pancake race in Olney. They set up a 415-yard course in Liberal, so today there are two Great Pancake Races — one in Olney and one in Liberal. At the end of both races, the towns call each other by trans-Atlantic telephone to see which town had the fastest runner.

What is the winner's trophy? It's a silver pancake griddle with the names of all the past winners engraved on it.

Food Time Capsule

Here is something special you can do with all the information you've been collecting about your food choices.

Make a Food Time Capsule that will be your very own. Put lots of things in it that show what's important to you about food and eating right now. You can use a small box like a shoe box. You may want to keep it a secret and not tell anyone what's inside yours. Tape it shut, mark the date on it, and put it away until at least the end of the year before you look at it again to see how your food tastes have changed.

Some things you might include:

- Photographs of your family meals on special occasions and on regular nights.
- A menu from your favorite restaurant (ask first).
- Your "Pick Your Favorites" chart.
- Special recipes — yours, your Mom's and Dad's, your grandmother's.
- A tape cassette of your family eating or mystery sounds of food cooking.
- A photo of you eating.
- Empty packages and wrappers from food you've eaten.
- A map of where your fruits and vegetables are coming from (include date, month, and year on this).
- Your "Spilling the Beans" story.
- An advertisement for a nutritious food.
- A list of foods you dislike.
- A page of supermarket ads.
- Your "Three Generation Questionnaire."

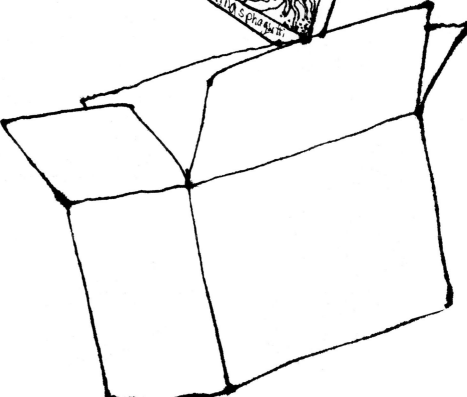

WHERE FOOD COMES FROM

Edible Plants — From Root to Fruit

It's time to sit down to another meal. What's on your plate today? Is it plant or animal? Some of those foods may not look at all like the plant or animal they came from, and you might like it that way. But have you ever thought about why those plants and animals on your plate make good foods — sources of *nutrients* like proteins and *carbohydrates* that help you grow and give you energy? Or do you wonder how those plants or animals got chosen as foods in the first place?

First, let's take a look at the plant foods on your plate. Maybe you have tomatoes and onions here, spaghetti there, with a little oregano and a bay leaf for taste. **Plants give us all the fruits, vegetables, herbs, spices, grains, and mushrooms we eat,** and that's quite a few. Man has eaten some 3,000 different plants through the ages, though only about 150 kinds of plants are now grown commercially for food.

How many different plants do you think you eat — 10, 20, 50? Start making a list. Some plant foods like carrots and potatoes are pretty obvious. But don't forget to count the pepper and other spices and herbs used to flavor your food, the wheat of your bread, and the corn oil margarine you spread on top of it. Take a close look at the ingredients on food package labels, too. You may be eating coconut oil in your crackers and not even know it.

Almost all the plant foods you eat come from flowering plants, except for the mushrooms in your soup, the yeasts in your high-rise bread, and the seaweed called algin in your ice cream. Flowering plants are all around you as house plants, trees, and the vegetables in your garden. Flowering plants can be as different as daffodils, oak trees, and broccoli. But **all flowering plants have the following parts: roots, stems, leaves, flowers, fruits, and seeds.** Each of these parts does a different job for the plant.

Green leaves like spinach are solar collectors. They capture the sun's energy and change it into food energy — the carbohydrate, sugar. This magical change depends on vitamins and minerals. So green leafy vegetables contain many of the vitamins and minerals that we need to stay healthy.

Sugar, the plant's energy for living, doesn't usually stay in

the leaves for long. It either gets used right away or is shipped through the stem to roots, fruits, or underground stems. One sweet apple gets its sugars from 15 to 35 leaves!

Stems such as asparagus are like a two-way street. They carry sugars down to feed the roots and bring up to the leaves the water and minerals needed to make more sugars. Certain plant stems like sugar cane store sugar. Underground stems like potatoes store their carbohydrates as starches.

The trunk of a maple tree is a stem, too. If you time it right, you can tap the trunks of New England maple trees in late winter to catch the sap as it heads upward. This sugary sap brings the buds energy for their springtime surge of growth.

The roots of plants like carrots are winter storehouses for the plant's food supply. They also absorb from the soil the water and minerals that the leaves need.

Not all roots are worth "rooting" for, though. Plants like carrots, beets, and parsnips are especially good food sources because they are *biennials.* That means they live for two growing seasons. The first spring, the seed grows only stems, leaves, and roots. At the end of its first growing season, the plant stores away its carbohydrates as starches in a large tasty *taproot.* Then in the second growing season, the biennial plant uses this stored starch energy to produce flowers and fruits.

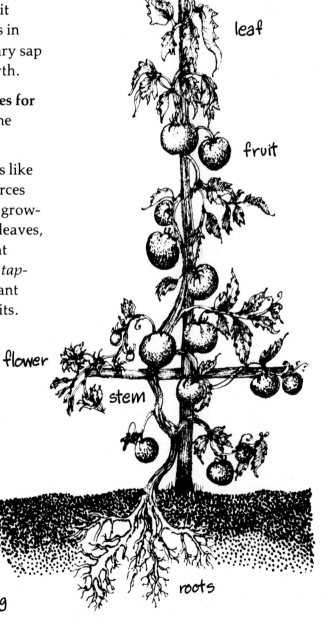

TOMATO PLANT

leaf

fruit

flower

stem

roots

CARROT at end of 1st growing season

CARROT at end of 2nd growing season

You may never have seen a carrot flower or fruit. That's because we usually dig up the large carrot root at the end of the first year before the plant has had a chance to use its stored energy.

The starch that stores the energy is a plant's way of saving space. It is made of hundreds of sugars joined together and *dehydrated* to save room. When the carrot plant needs energy, it adds water and changes starch back into sugars. Carrots from the garden taste sweeter in the second spring. That's when the starches are beginning to change back into sugars to give the plant energy for making flowers and fruits.

The flower is a plant's way of keeping the show going. In many plants, flowers put on colorful and fragrant displays that attract insects which then *pollinate* the flowers. Insects like the honeybee do this while searching for nectar hidden in the flower. As they search, they pick up pollen on their bodies and carry it with them from flower to flower.

Most flowers have to be pollinated before they can produce fruits and seeds. If there are too many rainy days while the apple blossoms are out, the bees can't do their work. And less pollination of apple flowers means fewer apples on each tree. Rain every day keeps the apples away!

Flowers' nectar provides food for honeybees who eventually pass it along to us as honey. Sometimes we eat the flowers themselves. Take a closer look at your broccoli next time. You'll find hundreds of tiny green flowers at the end of each stalk. And keep an eye out for cauliflower and artichokes — they're flowers too.

BROCCOLI

A SWEET STORY

It takes 160,000 honeybees to make a pound of honey. Each honeybee carries only a teaspoonful of nectar to the hive during its 4 to 6 week life. Four pounds of nectar from some 2 million flowers make one pound of honey. Eighty thousand bees are needed to bring that much nectar to the hive and 80,000 more wave their wings to evaporate the nectar into one pound of honey. (If you want your honey bottled, it may take

40,000 more honey bees — 20,000 to hold the bottle and 20,000 to screw on the lid!) _____

After the flowers have been pollinated, they lose their petals and develop into fruits. Depending on the plant, they can become fruits like apples or cherries, grapes or coconuts, strawberries or blueberries or tomatoes. Tomatoes? Yes — tomatoes are really fruits too, though we call them vegetables.

Back in 1893, the United States Supreme Court declared that the tomato is a vegetable because it is usually eaten as part of a meal's main course. Any plant part that is eaten as an appetizer, dessert, or out-of-hand was labeled a fruit. So legally a tomato is a vegetable, even though it is the fruit of a plant.

Fruits are a plant's way of getting around. Fruits contain the seeds of a plant. They protect these seeds and help transport them away from the parent plant. Fruits like apples, peaches, and pears have a sweet fleshy outer coat that surrounds the seeds. These fruits contain stored starch carbohydrates which turn into sweet sugars as the fruit ripens.

Birds and mammals can't resist these sweet tasty bribes. Animals often help plants by eating their seeds. As animals eat the fruits and move elsewhere, the seeds take a trip through their digestive tracts. Many seeds *need* a trip through an animal's digestive tract to weaken their tough seed coats, so they can sprout or germinate. As the seeds complete their trip through the animal, they are usually dropped in a new spot and given a pile of fertilizer as a going-away present!

Seeds are the plant's future. Each seed contains an embryo (baby) plant with its own built-in food supply of proteins, oils, and starches. There is just enough food to keep the embryo going until it can grow leaves and capture its own solar energy to make its own food.

Seeds are an especially good source of nutrients for this reason. We eat plenty of them — peanuts, beans, nuts, and grains like wheat, rice, and corn. Protein is a very important nutrient for building bodies — both plants' and yours. And seeds are the best source of protein in the plant world.

DON'T SIT THERE LIKE A VEGETABLE!

Do you know which of these vegetables are really the fruits of plants? Write your answers on a separate sheet of paper.

green pepper	carrot
pea pod	eggplant
cucumber	potato
lettuce	avocado
onion	broccoli
string bean	cabbage
cauliflower	zucchini
corn	

(See page 210 for the answers.)

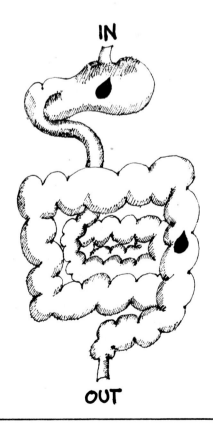

IN

OUT

PEANUT EMBRYO

Take a shelled peanut. Remove the skin and carefully separate the two halves. Inside you will find the plant embryo - its leaves and root - and its food supply.

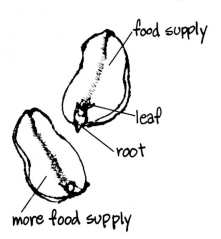

food supply

leaf

root

more food supply

Seeds also contain a concentrated energy source in their oils. Seed oils like corn, peanut, and olive oil are liquid fats that give more than twice as much energy as the same amount of carbohydrate (starch or sugar) or protein. That's especially important if you live in a cold place with a polar bear as a neighbor and needs lot of energy to stay warm. If you don't, and you eat lots of oily seeds anyway without burning off that energy, you may begin to *look* like a polar bear.

Some seeds are better food sources than others. Two-thirds of the world's population depends on seeds from the grass family for its main diet. The grains we eat are seeds from special grasses like wheat, rice, rye, and oats, that are called *annuals.* These grasses live for only one year, produce seeds, and die.

We don't eat the seeds of grasses like the Kentucky Blue Grass or crabgrass of your front lawn. Their seeds are too small. These plants are *perennials.* This means that they live for several years. They survive winters by storing their food below ground in roots and underground stems. They don't put all their nutrients into their seeds as the annual grasses do. This means that large annual grass seeds make a better food source for us than the smaller perennial grass seeds. Small perennial grass seeds aren't worth our effort to collect — but they do make good snacks for mice.

Any plant that is the main source of food for a group of people is called a *staple.* The staple food crops in most parts of the world are grains like wheat and rice, and "root" crops like yams, potatoes, and sweet potatoes (crops, you remember, which are really underground stems). The seed foods contain valuable protein as well as a concentrated energy supply. "Root" crops have lots of water compared to the amount of nutrients they contain.

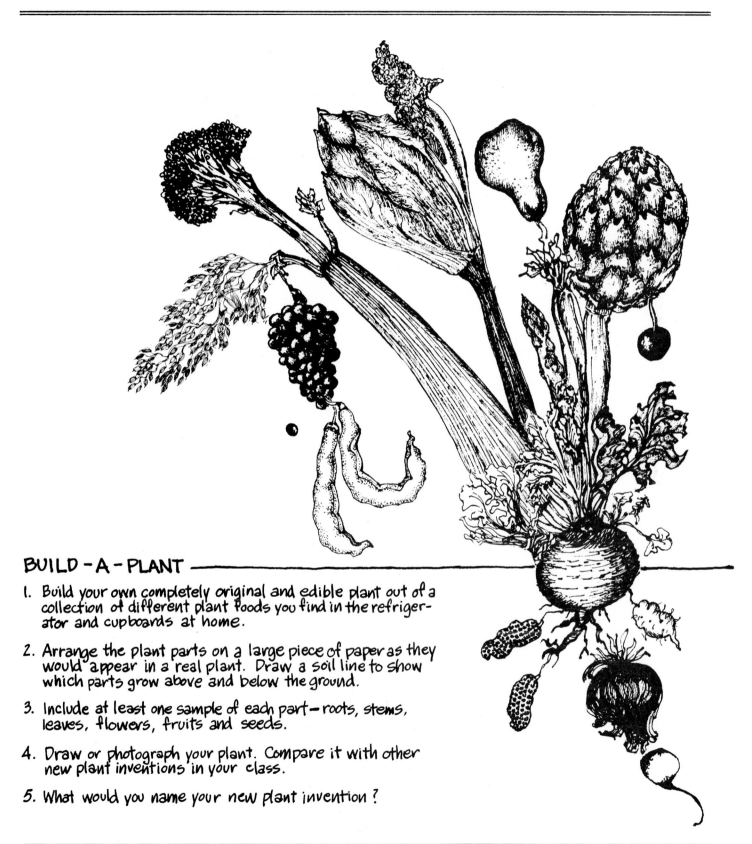

BUILD – A – PLANT

1. Build your own completely original and edible plant out of a collection of different plant foods you find in the refrigerator and cupboards at home.

2. Arrange the plant parts on a large piece of paper as they would appear in a real plant. Draw a soil line to show which parts grow above and below the ground.

3. Include at least one sample of each part—roots, stems, leaves, flowers, fruits and seeds.

4. Draw or photograph your plant. Compare it with other new plant inventions in your class.

5. What would you name your new plant invention?

PLANT PART CHART

Plant Part	Food
Leaf	spinach, lettuce, cabbage, chives, parsley
Stems:	
Leaf stem (petiole)	celery, rhubarb
Plant stem	asparagus, bamboo, sugar cane
Underground stem	potato, ginger, sweet potato, yam, Jerusalem artichoke
Root	carrot, radish, turnip, beet, parsnip
Flower	artichoke, broccoli, cauliflower
Fruit	apple, avocado, banana, coconut, corn, cucumber, eggplant, green pepper, orange, peppercorn, pineapple, squash, strawberry, stringbean, tomato, watermelon
Seed	peanut, walnut, popcorn, lima bean, pea, sunflower, rye, wheat, rice, sesame
Bulb (underground stem and leaves)	onion, garlic

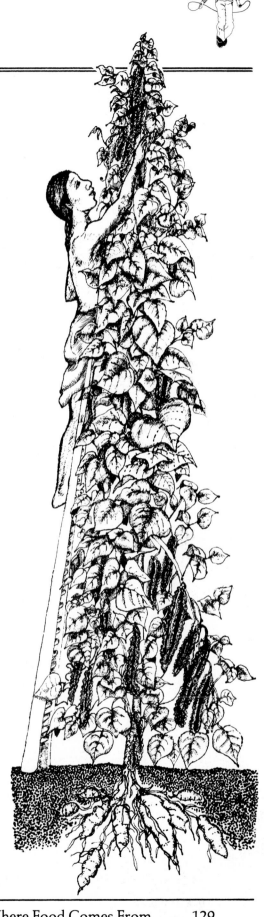

You may eat some other plant parts as well. The spice cinnamon, for example, is the bark of a tree, and cloves are dried tree flower buds.

Not all parts of each plant are edible. The part you can eat is different in different kinds of plants. In rhubarb you can eat the stem, but the leaves are poisonous. Apples are tasty, but the seeds contain the poison cyanide. In most plants you can eat just one part, but in some you can eat several. Broccoli lovers eat flowers, stems, and leaves.

There is one plant from which you can eat almost every part — the winged bean.

THE WONDERFUL WINGED BEAN

The amazing winged bean plant is like having peanuts, peapods, potatoes, spinach, and cauliflower all rolled into one plant! The winged bean is a 12-foot-high plant that grows in backyard gardens in the tropics of New Guinea and Southeast Asia. Every part of this plant is edible except the roots.

Its young, winged green **pods** and **shoots** are tender crunchy vegetables. Its **seeds** are roasted and eaten like peanuts. The bulbous **underground stems** are eaten like potatoes, boiled or baked in a fire while wrapped in banana leaves. The **leaves** and **flowers** are eaten in salads or soups, raw or cooked. All the parts of this incredible plant are rich in protein, vitamins and minerals.

There are a great number of winged bean varieties (over 100). Some of them are important parts of tribal ceremonies. Although the winged bean has probably been cultivated in New Guinea for hundreds of years, scientists have only recently discovered it. It is an important protein crop that could save people in other tropical countries from *protein deficiency* and *malnutrition.* _____

Where Do Plant Foods Store Their Nutrients?

Test two of each kind of plant part to find out. Use stems, roots, leaves, flowers, fruits, and seeds.

Fat test

1. Cut up a large paper bag to make a flat sheet of paper.

2. Rub each food to be tested on a different spot of paper. Circle the spot and write the food name near each spot.

3. Let the paper dry in the sun or over a radiator.

4. Hold the paper up to the light. Where fat is present, the light will show through.

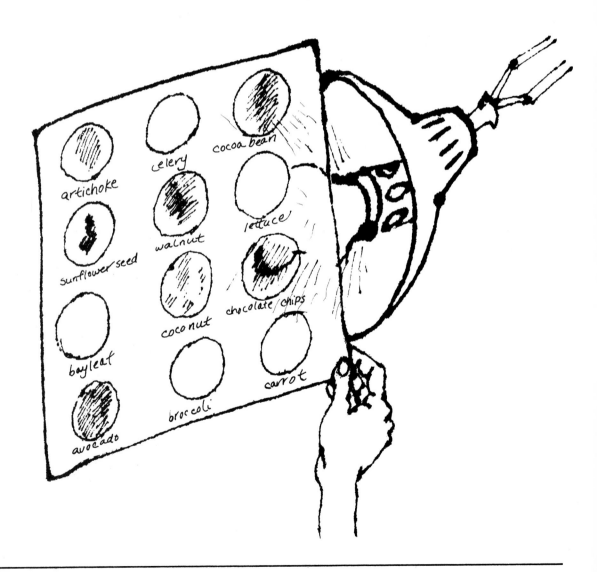

Starch Test

1. Get some tincture of iodine from the drugstore or medicine chest.

2. Add a drop of iodine to each food to be tested.

3. If starch is present, the iodine will change from reddish-brown to bluish-black.

4. Throw away all the food you tested. **Iodine is poisonous.**

Results

Make a chart like this to keep track of your results.

FOOD	PLANT PART	STARCH	FAT
carrot	root	yes	no

1. What nutrients did you find in roots, stems, leaves, flowers, fruits, and seeds?

    Do all roots contain the same nutrients?

    What about the other plant parts?

2. Compare your results with a friend who tested different fruits and vegetables.

Plant Your Leftovers

Seeds

Here's something to do with the seedy characters around your house.

1. Save the seeds from your orange, grapefruit, apple, watermelon, squash, or green pepper. Collect seeds from any foods you eat.

2. Wash the pulp off of the seeds. If you can't use the seeds right away, dry them and save for later.

3. When you're ready to plant, soak them in water overnight.

4. Plant them in a container of potting soil. Cottage cheese containers or school milk containers work well. Plant the seeds 1/4 inch deep and at least one inch apart.

5. Moisten the soil and put the container in a warm place. Make sure the soil remains moist but not drenched.

6. Watch for seedlings. When they are at least an inch high, replant them in a larger container of soil. Put them in a sunny spot.

Roots

If you dig carrots, try this.

1. Take a good-sized fat carrot. Cut off 2 inches from the fat end of the carrot and save it. (Eat the other end.)

2. From the end you cut, carefully scoop out the carrot's insides so that you have a leakproof shell. An apple corer or vegetable peeler may be helpful for this. Hollow out your carrot enough to hold a teaspoon or two of water.

3. Fill your carrot with water. Poke three toothpicks into your root. Tie a string to each toothpick and hang your carrot in a sunny window. Keep the hole filled with water. Watch for green shoots growing from the carrot's top. (If beets or turnips are your dish, try this experiment with one of them.)

Underground Stems (Tubers)

If your potato starts to give you the eye, it's time to plant it.

1. Cut out a section of the potato with an eye. (The eye of a potato is a stem and leaf bud.)

2. Place this potato section on top of damp sand in a small container.

3. Cover the container with a lid or plastic bag. Put it in a dark place until your potato sprouts.

4. Remove the cover and put the container in a sunny spot.

5. As the potato plant grows larger, replant it in potting soil in a larger container or in a garden.

Cultivating Your Tastes

Although there are over 300,000 plant species known in the world today, only 150 of them are grown commercially as food. How did those lucky 150 get chosen as food for man? We know that more than 10,000 years ago, the first people were hunters and plant gatherers. They roamed the land, following animal herds and gathering edible parts of wild plants. If they watched carefully, they found out by other people's mistakes which plants were poisonous, and lived to pick another day.

People who carried seeds back to their homes noticed that the seeds they accidentally dropped nearby sometimes took root and grew. These people learned to sow seeds and take care of the plants. They became the first farmers.

Archaeologists have found ancient plant carvings in stone, and the remains of ancient seeds in Egypt and China. From these, we know that plants like wheat, barley, and rice have been cultivated for thousands of years. In 1970, an archaeological find at "Spirit Cave" in Thailand uncovered cultivated seeds of peas, beans, cucumbers, and water chestnuts that are at least 10,000 years old.

As people began to cultivate food plants near their homes, they produced a larger food supply which allowed them to end their daily wanderings and gather together in groups. Twenty square kilometers are needed to support one single plant gatherer. The same area under modern cultivation can feed 6,000 people.

Although most of the world's population today depends on cultivated plants as foods, we still harvest some wild plants. Who can resist ripe blueberries or wild raspberries on a summer day? Some folks tap trees for maple syrup or collect wild edible weeds. The Indians showed the colonists how to gather wild young milkweed pods, early dandelion greens, and pokewood shoots. Without these wild plants, the settlers would never have gotten through the days of early spring, when their root-cellars were almost empty and the new crops had not yet come up.

A Spicy Story

The plants we call food have traveled incredible distances and have amazing tales to tell of their adventures. **Spices like pepper, ginger, cloves, and cinnamon were very important plants in past history.** Kings sent expeditions in search of them, merchants risked their lives and fortunes, and wars were fought over them. Why? Because for centuries there was no refrigeration, and fresh meat spoiled quickly. Strong spices improved the flavor of slightly rotten food. Some, like cinnamon and rosemary, helped to preserve foods. They were also used as incense to cover up unpleasant smells, and to embalm dead bodies.

Spices cost a lot because they came from far-off lands in the East. Long overland journeys or sea voyages lasting months or even years were required to obtain them. In the Middle Ages, more than 1,000 years ago, pepper was as valued as diamonds and as sought-after as gold. It was so valuable that peppercorns were used as money for paying rent and taxes.

SPICE SEARCH

Look through all the whole spices and herbs in your cupboard. Try to figure out what plant parts they come from:

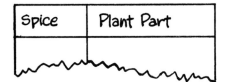

Spice	Plant Part

"how much do I owe you?"

NOTHING TO SNEEZE AT

Salem, Massachusetts, was the center of the pepper trade in the 1800's. Captain Jonathan Carnes of the schooner "Rajah" left Salem harbor on a secret voyage in November, 1795. He went 24,000 miles in 18 months and returned from the island of Sumatra in Southeast Asia with a cargo of peppercorns that earned the owners thousands of dollars — 700 times the amount of money they spent for the voyage. In 1805, Salem exported 7 million pounds of pepper to the countries of the world.

EXPENSIVE TASTES

Today's most expensive spice is saffron. Saffron is used to flavor and color rice dishes in many parts of the world. It comes from the three-part *stigma* of the Spanish crocus flower. It takes 96,000 stigmas, hand-picked from 32,000 crocus flowers, to make one pound of saffron. Saffron sells for almost $900 per pound today!

Columbus discovered America because of spices. He was looking for a direct sea route to the spice sources in India and the Orient and bumped into America instead. Although Columbus couldn't bring spices back to Queen Isabella, he did bring back Indian corn, beginning an exchange of fruits and vegetables between continents that continued with every new explorer.

stigma

Vegetable and Fruit Travelers

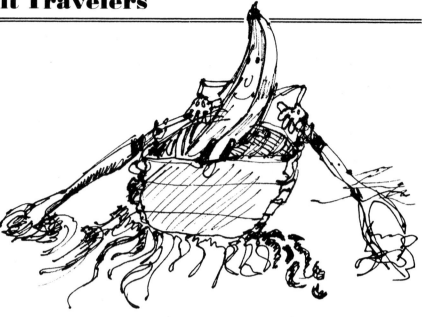

So many food plants have traveled around the world that the only native North American fruits and vegetables we eat today are corn, beans, sweet potato, red and green peppers, squash, pumpkin, and Jerusalem artichoke. Foods like potatoes, peanuts, and tomatoes got their start in South America, made their way to Europe and Africa with the Spanish explorers, and then found their way back to North America.

TALE OF A TOMATO

Tomatoes were first cultivated in the Andes mountains of South America. The Spanish explorers brought tomato seeds back to Spain. From there they spread to Italy. The Italians started growing tomatoes in 1530 and were the first Europeans to eat them. Twenty-five years later, the English and Spanish were still growing tomatoes in their gardens only for show.

In 1781, Thomas Jefferson grew tomatoes as food in his garden, but most Americans, especially those in the Northeast, refused to eat them. They thought tomatoes were poisonous because they belonged to the Deadly Nightshade plant family.

In 1839, Colonel Robert Johnson stood on the steps of a New Jersey courthouse and ate a "poisonous" red, raw tomato in front of a shocked crowd. The crowd stood by and waited for Johnson to die. They were disappointed. He survived, and

eventually the tomato gained in popularity. By shortly after the Civil War, Americans were eating tomatoes in huge quantities. _____

PATH OF A POTATO
(POTATOES COME OUT FROM UNDER)

Potatoes, known as batatas or patatas, were grown and eaten by the Indians in South America 2,000 years ago. These early potatoes were the size and shape of peanuts. The Indians soaked the potatoes in water, let them freeze in the cold mountain air, and dried them in the warm sun to produce the first freeze-dried potatoes. Then they walked on the potatoes with their bare feet to rub off the skins. The potatoes turned black and hard. They were then resoaked and used for food until the next potato harvest.

Pizarro, the Spanish conquerer, brought the potato home to Spain in 1539. But like its cousin the tomato, the potato had a tough time being accepted as a food. In some countries of Europe, a few daring people ate potatoes, but most folks thought them dangerous. Green potatoes, potatoes that have been lying in the sun, are poisonous. But white potatoes are not.

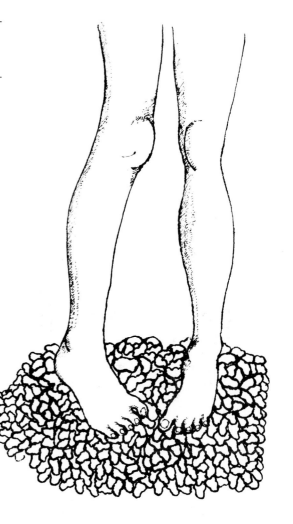

The Irish were one people who quickly caught on to the potato as a valuable food source, and by the 1600's it had become their main food. However, an epidemic of potato blight disease in the 1840's caused a serious famine in Ireland, during which thousands of people died, and 3 million Irish people moved to the United States.

Americans didn't eat potatoes until 1719, when early Irish immigrants brought them to Londonderry, New Hampshire. Now the average American eats 65 pounds of potatoes a year.

THE PEANUT - GOOBER'S GOINGS

Peanuts, also called "goober's peas" or "ground nuts," are another South American plant cultivated by the Indians 2,000 years ago. The Spanish discovered the peanut in the 1400's and

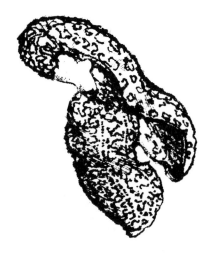

brought it to Europe, Africa, and the Orient. The peanut then made its way back to North America from Africa as food for slaves on the early slave ships. Because of those journeys on slave ships, peanuts were not popular as food for either the slaves or their masters.

Peanuts were grown as flower curiosities in Virginia and North Carolina. The flower of the peanut plant bends to the ground after pollination and pushes underground, where the seeds of the peanut fruit ripen in their papery shells.

PEANUT PLANT

It was not until the Civil War that Confederate soldiers discovered how good goober peas were roasted in an open fire. A popular Confederate song of the war was called "Goober Peas." The composer was a Mr. P. Nutt.

Dr. George Washington Carver, a Black botanist, was the man who discovered that peanuts were good for more than food. He developed some 300 products from the peanut plant, including ink, industrial diamonds, shampoo, and shaving cream.

And, in 1890, a St. Louis doctor invented peanut butter, so that the peanut spread even further! _____

THE APPLE OF YOUR EYE (HOW DO YOU LIKE THEM APPLES?)

The apple's ancestors grew more than 5,000 years ago in Southeast Asia before they spread to Europe. Five-thousand-year-old fossils of apples have been found embedded in the mud at the bottom of Swiss lakes. In Norway, an excavated Viking ship contained a bucket of apples, wrinkled and brown, that were picked and packed over 1,000 years before.

The early colonists brought apples to America in the 1600's. In the 1800's, a fellow named John Chapman, from Leominster, Massachusetts, collected apple seeds from cider mills, dried them, and put them in little bags. He gave them to everyone he met as he headed west. For forty years, this missionary, known as "Johnny Appleseed," traveled by horse and wagon and canoe. He carried his Bible in hand and wore his cooking pot on his head as he journeyed through Ohio, Illinois, and Iowa, planting apple seeds as he went. Many of the grandchildren of these seeds are still bearing fruit today.

There are more than 6,500 apple varieties in the world, 1,000 of these in the United States. Every region has its local favorites. In New England, three out of every four apples grown are McIntosh apples. These are all descendants of the apple tree John McIntosh found near his house in Ontario, Canada, in 1796. The McIntosh tree lived until 1908 and bore fruit for 112 years. John McIntosh spread the apple variety that bears his name by giving cuttings of branches to his friends and neighbors.

All of today's familiar apple varieties are spread the same way — by grafting (joining) the branches of special tasty varieties to the stem and roots of other kinds of apple trees. Planting apples from seed is fine if you like surprises. The baby plant has two parents and shows some characteristics of each. You can never tell whether or not an apple tree will get its mother's hardy roots or its father's tasty fruits. _____

The New Breed

Most plant foods of today in search of their "roots" would find very different looking and tasting ancestors in their pasts. Long ago people learned to choose plants whose fruits and vegetables were the biggest and best tasting. They saved those seeds to plant and threw away or ate the rest. Thousands of years of this kind of choosing have produced plants that have larger and fleshier roots, stronger stems, larger flowers, fruits, and seeds, and more fruits and seeds than their ancestors.

Nature has done her own share of creating new varieties by *cross-pollination* of flowers. Wind and insects often carry pollen from flower to flower, sometimes making new plant combinations. But man has sped up this process in his role as a giant bee, making crosses between different plant varieties.

Plants are now bred for more than size, taste, and their ability to produce lots of fruits and seeds. They are also bred for resistance to disease, for firm fruits that can survive long truck journeys, for stalks and fruits that make them easier to harvest by machinery, and for longer shelf-life and more appealing colors.

But taste and color don't always win. Think of the difference between the juicy, sweet summer garden-grown tomatoes and the firm, pale, and tasteless supermarket tomatoes that travel from winter greenhouse or faraway fields. The supermarket variety needs tougher skins to travel in and must be picked before it's ripe.

PLANT WIZARD

Luther Burbank was born in 1849 in Lancaster, Massachusetts. At the age of 22, he bought a small 17-acre plot and began a truck garden. He grew vegetables to sell in nearby Fitchburg. But he had lots of competition in the vegetable business, so he began experimenting with his plants. He wanted to raise better vegetables than his competitors and to get them to market ahead of the others.

He kept track of all his plants that produced bigger or better vegetables. He watched for tastier fruits and for fruits that ripened early. He kept the seeds of these outstanding plants for his next year's crop.

Three years later, he developed the famous Russet Burbank potato, which even now is the most widely grown potato in the U.S. He sold his amazing potato for $150 and headed west to California.

In 1877, he began his own nursery business. That year, he made only $15.20. He imported new plants from Japan and continued experimenting with plant crosses to produce new varieties. His nursery business picked up, until in 1884, only seven years after he started, he made over $10,000!

Luther Burbank went on to create a white blackberry, a spineless cactus, and a plumcot (a cross between an apricot and a plum). He introduced over 800 new varieties of plants in his lifetime, including 66 new kinds of fruits, nine new vegetables, and seven new nut trees. What a wizard he was! _____

A FRUIT AND VEGETABLE WISH FOR YOUR DISH

1. Make up your own new fruit and vegetable inventions.

2. What new kinds of fruit and vegetables would you breed that might sell? Would you create celery without the strings or onions without the tears?

3. How would that new fruit or vegetable convince someone to buy it? Write a story that explains how.

Here are some new fruit and vegetables models which have already been developed:

Plant	Characteristics Bred For
Tomato	Fruits with less acid Larger fruits with more pulp and fewer seeds Firm fruits that don't spoil with handling
Carrot	Larger and sweeter roots
Cucumber	Less bitter fruits Seedless fruits "Burpless" fruits
Peas	Pods that grow concentrated at the top of the plant and pods that ripen all at the same time, to make harvesting easier
Sugarbeet	Higher sugar content in roots
Orange	Seedless fruits
Watermelon	Square fruits that are easier to transport and fit into a refrigerator

ORANGE YOU SURPRISED?

Two hundred years ago, an orange-picker in Brazil noticed an orange tree with big funny-looking fruits. Each fruit had a large bump on one end. He cut open an orange and tasted it. It was sweet and juicy and had no seeds. Each fruit was a double orange with a small fruit growing out of a large one — making a bump that looked like a belly-button or navel. He cut buds from the branches and grew more of these navel oranges. (Like apple trees, special orange tree varieties can only be spread by branch cuttings or buds, not by seeds.)

One hundred years passed, and a woman traveler from the United States saw navel oranges growing in Brazil. She sent some budded cuttings to the Department of Agriculture in Washington. In 1879, Mrs. Tibbets of Riverside, California, visited Washington and brought home three of these orange buds.

She planted the budded trees near the back door of her farmhouse. When rain was scarce, Mrs. Tibbets watered them with her dishwater. The trees did well, and five years later they bore their first fruit — the first of the famous California navel oranges. One of her original orange trees still stands in Riverside today — now over 100 years old.

Saving for a Rainy Day

Today there are only 20 major plant foods that feed most of the world's population, and these crops come from very few varieties of plants. Plants of the same variety may all be susceptible to the same insect pests or diseases. This means that all the corn or wheat crops of a certain variety could be wiped out at once. It's like putting all your eggs in one basket. If anything happens to that basket. . .! The United States has decided to put some seeds away in a bank just in case. The National Seed Storage Laboratory in Fort Collins, Colorado, has 100,000 different seeds stored away, including little used *species* and the wild relatives of cultivated species. That should make you rest easier.

THE WORLD'S 20 MAJOR FOOD CROPS

potatoes	oats
sweet potatoes	barley
tomatoes	buckwheat
beans	millet
peas	sorghum
peanuts	sugar cane
soy beans	sugar beets
corn	coconuts
wheat	bananas
rice	tapioca

Animal Foods — Back to Home Plate

Let's take another look at your plate. Push aside all those roots and fruits for a moment. How many different animals are on your plate? Most of our animal food comes from eggs and milk, and from the meat of cattle, pig, lamb, chicken, turkey, and fish. Folks around the world may also fill their plates with frogs, snails, insects, snakes, and a wide variety of different birds and animals. Americans no longer eat robin pie, but it was popular in the early 1800's.

Throughout much of our history, we depended on hunting, fishing, and plant gathering. Cave paintings in southern France that are 40,000 years old show the bison and tigers that were probably the meals of these early cave people. At least some 10,000 years ago, man began to keep herds and flocks nearby and settled down into villages. Since that time, many folks have raised domestic animals as food. For 4,000 years, Peruvians have raised guinea pigs for meat. The reindeer, water-buffalo, and yak have all had their place on the plate, too.

What does all this meat have to offer us in the way of food? Mostly we eat the muscles of animals. We also drink the milk of mammals such as cow, goat, and man (woman!) and eat the eggs of chicken and fish (caviar).

A Place in the Sun — The Food Chain

All the plants and animals we eat are part of a food chain. Remember that the sun's energy is captured by green plants which change it into the food energy of carbohydrates, fats, and proteins. Then animals (like us) eat green plants to get their energy, or else they eat the animals that ate the plants. And the chain may keep on going. There may be five links if the animal at the top of the food chain is four animals up the line from the plant eater. (If an animal ate an animal who ate an animal who ate an animal who ate an animal who ate a plant!)

The name of the game is energy loss. Along every step of the food chain, most of the sun's energy (90 percent of it) gets lost as heat. This happens as food energy is passed from plant to animal, and from animal to animal. Only a very small amount of energy (the remaining 10 percent) is stored in plant and animal tissues. This stored energy can be used by other

animals as food.

The further up the food chain you eat, the more energy gets lost as heat along the way. Eating an animal like cattle is like "eating sunshine" third-hand. This means that it costs more of the sun's energy to eat animal foods than plant foods.

Only green plants can capture the sun's energy, and the world has a shrinking amount of farmland on which to grow those green plants. So, we need to think more carefully about *where* we eat in the food chain. **One acre of corn can feed twenty times more men than one acre of corn used to raise animals for meat.** That is a pretty important fact with 4 billion people in the world to feed and a limited amount of farmland. Most of the world's population depends almost entirely on plant foods for their daily diet. Do you?

I acre of corn
will feed
1000 people for 1 day —

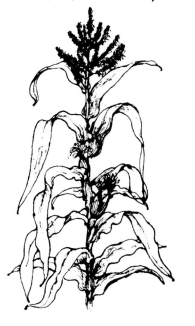

I acre of corn
fed to cattle
eaten as meat
will feed
50 people for 1 day —

Protein Machines

How well do animals do as "protein machines"? How much food do they need to eat to produce protein that we can use?

Cattle grazing on grass are able to take plants that would be indigestible to us and turn them into protein. They do this by the churning magic of their special four-part ruminant stomachs. The huge first stomach, or rumen, of cattle contains microscopic organisms that do the job.

But most cattle today are not home on the range eating grass. They are in feedlots instead, eating grains which we could easily digest ourselves.

Cattle feedlots hold up to 100,000 head of cattle in small pens. Cattle arrive at the feedlot weighing 600 to 750 pounds. They gain an average of two pounds a day eating a grain diet, adding some 600 pounds in 300 days before they go to market.

Feedlot beef is more marbled with fat and more tender than grass-fed beef. This is because feedlot cattle get very little exercise. Their roaming cousins get a lot more exercise grazing. So grass-fed beef has more muscle (protein) than fat.

The feedlot beef cattle have to eat 21 pounds of protein in order to give us one pound of protein we can eat. That's like paying $21 to get $1 in return. How well do you think other animals do as protein machines?

On the next page, you can see how many pounds of plant protein animals must eat in order to give us one pound of animal protein.

PROTEIN CONSUMPTION

Beef consumption in the United States increased from 64 pounds per person in 1960 to 96 pounds per person in 1976.

1960   1976

Chicken consumption is up from 28 pounds per person in 1960 to 43 pounds per person in 1976.

1960   1976

And fish consumption rose from 4 pounds per person in 1960 to almost 6 pounds per person in 1976.

1960   1976

PROTEIN MACHINES

☼ = 1 pound of plant protein

= 1 pound of animal protein

Cattle eat
21.4 pounds of
plant protein

Pigs eat
8.3 pounds of
plant protein

Chickens and
turkeys eat
5.5 pounds of
plant protein

Cows eat
4.4 pounds of
plant protein

Hens eat
4.3 pounds of
plant protein

to produce
1 pound of
animal protein

to produce
1 pound of
animal protein

to produce
1 pound of
animal protein

to produce
1 pound of
animal protein

to produce
1 pound of
animal protein

PROTEIN QUEEN

A 9½-year-old Holstein Cow named Mowry Prince Corinne from Roaring Springs, Pennsylvania, holds the record as "milk machine." The average United States cow produces 4,200 quarts of milk a year. Mowry Prince Corinne produced almost *24,000 quarts* in one year — enough milk to supply 64 families for a year! On her highest day, she produced almost 90 quarts of milk.

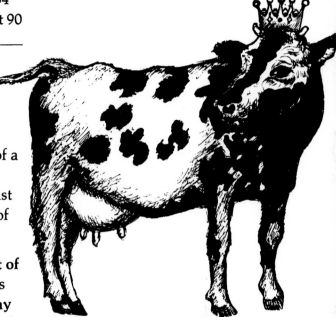

Scientific breeding of animals began in the late 1800's. Average modern cows give ten times more milk than cows of a century ago, and hens lay up to four times as many eggs (an average of 315 eggs per year). Beef is ready for market at least three years sooner than it used to be. But our consumption of animal protein has increased too.

As average Americans, we eat almost twice the amount of protein we need for body growth and repair. Extra protein is used to provide body energy. But **protein is an expensive way to get energy,** when carbohydrates like fruits, vegetables, and grains are so inexpensive and so easily available.

The Food Chain Grows

Modern man has added a few new links to nature's food chain. Food now often goes through many steps from the field or feedlot to your table. Food may be grown using energy-consuming fertilizers, harvested by machinery, and factory processed to add or remove ingredients. This food may then be canned, bottled, frozen, or packaged, so that it can be transported long distances by truck or train to you.

Like the food chain in nature, each of these steps uses up energy. **The more steps a food goes through from field to table, the more energy, petroleum or electrical, is lost along the way.**

Stashing the Goods

Fresh food doesn't last long. The air and water everywhere are filled with microorganisms like bacteria, yeasts, and molds, which need moisture, warmth, and a food supply to grow. Fresh food provides a perfect home for these critters who spoil the food for our use, and some may even poison us in the process.

There are a number of ways to preserve foods from this spoilage:

- You can destroy the microorganisms with **heat.** Most are killed at temperatures between 140° F. and 190° F., except for the deadly botulism bacteria which can survive in temperatures up to 250° F.

- You can **remove the moisture** that bacteria and molds need to live. Dehydration, freeze-drying, salting, and pickling foods do this.

- You can stop the growth of microorganisms by **freezing** and holding foods at temperatures of 0° F.

Drying

This is an old method, as it requires only sun. Many dehydrated foods today, however, take a trip through air-blown ovens. Removing the water slows the growth of bacteria and molds. Food is lighter and smaller and easier to store.

Pickling and Salting

Pickling creates an acid *environment* that is not friendly towards microorganisms. It also creates a salty environment which draws the water out of the bacteria and molds so they can't live to spoil your food.

Salting does the same thing — removes the moisture.

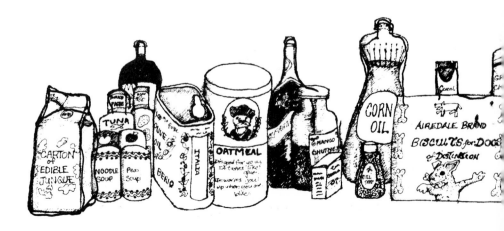

Freeze-Drying

In freeze-drying, food is kept frozen while it dries in a *vacuum*. This keeps water from the microorganisms and causes much less shrinkage than ordinary drying. A freeze-dried strawberry is as large as a fresh strawberry but weighs only 1/16 as much. Freeze-dried foods come in handy when you're backpacking or camping and don't want to carry the extra weight of water.

Canning

Heating foods to very high temperatures to destroy bacteria and molds and then sealing them in glass or metal containers keeps food from spoiling. Nicolas Appert, a French chef, invented canning in 1809. Napoleon had offered a generous prize to the person who could figure out a way to supply his soldiers with preserved foods. Nicolas won the prize.

These different ways of preserving foods use different amounts of energy in the process.

Compare the amount of energy these three ways of preserving fruits and vegetables use compared to the energy used in producing fresh fruits and vegetables.

Imagine a restaurant called "Petroleum Palace" where the price of food served was determined only by the amount of energy that food took to be *produced*, *processed*, and *transported* to your plate. Foods that use a lot of energy would cost more than those that use less energy.

If you wanted to pick a dinner that saved energy and money, would you choose fresh or frozen carrots as your vegetable? Which would cost less, a grain- or grass-fed beef hamburger? And what beverage would be the better energy bargain, juice in an aluminum can or juice in a returnable glass bottle?

AMOUNT OF ENERGY USED TO PRESERVE FRUITS AND VEGETABLES

FRESH REFRIGERATED:

1.07 kilowatt hours✳ per pound

CANNED:

1.76 kilowatt hours✳ per pound

FROZEN:

2.53 kilowatt hours✳ per pound

DEHYDRATED:

3.16 kilowatt hours✳ per pound

✳ One kilowatt hour will light a 100 watt bulb for 10 hours.

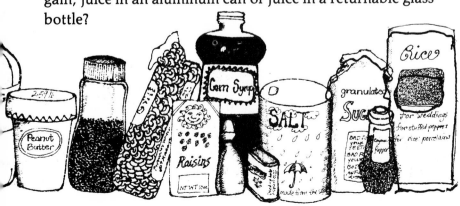

NUTRITION: THE INSIDE STORY

Does Your Food Fit?

"You wear your food well!" That could mean you just missed your mouth and a forkful of spaghetti is dripping down the front of your shirt. But you also wear your food in another way. The food you eat builds your body and keeps it growing and going.

Your body is made up of millions of tiny cells that need food to live. The way these cells are arranged in the tissues and organs of your body stays the same throughout your life. But most of the parts — the cells — are constantly being replaced. The skin that covers your body today is not the same skin that covered you seven years ago. It's made of completely new cells. Your oldest red blood cell is celebrating its four-month birthday, and the lining of your digestive tract is only three days old — the oldest it will ever get.

To keep your body going, you have to continuously replace the cells that wear out. That's where food comes into the picture. The steady stream of food you swallow throughout your life — some 50 tons of food and 10,000 gallons of fluid — provides these replacement parts, along with the energy that puts them all together and keeps them working.

That doesn't mean you are exactly the spaghetti or salad you ate last night. Food must be taken apart and rearranged before its pieces can be used to make the parts of your body — your skin, bones, muscles, and blood.

You eat foods, but what you take from them is some 50 known *nutrients*. **Nutrients are substances in foods that are used to help your body grow and repair itself.** The foods you eat are taken apart (digested), and the nutrients are then rearranged to make up the special body that is you. The science of *nutrition* is the study of the nutrients in food and how your body handles them.

All 50 nutrients contained in foods can be grouped into six categories: carbohydrates, fats, proteins, water, vitamins, and minerals. They are much easier to remember that way. Foods are usually a combination of nutrients. For example, a potato contains carbohydrates, proteins, water, vitamins, and minerals.

Are Carbohydrates "Fuelish?"

Carbohydrates are an important group of energy nutrients. They are the starches and sugars that give your body much of the fuel it needs for living. Most carbohydrates come from plant foods.

CARBOHYDRATE FOOD SOURCES

Starches
Grains and grain products
Legumes (dry peas and beans)
Vegetables like potatoes
    and corn

Sugars
Fruits like plums and apples
Vegetables like sweet
    potatoes and tomatoes
Table sugar (from sugar beet
    or sugar cane)
Honey
Milk (lactose)

Energy to Burn

Starches and sugars have the reputation of being fattening because of the calories (energy) they give your body when burned. But carbohydrates are no more fattening than proteins and less fattening than fats.

An equal amount of carbohydrate and protein (1 gram) will give you the same number of calories (4 Calories). The same amount of fat will give you more than twice the number of calories (9 Calories) as carbohydrate and protein. But none of these nutrients is fattening unless you eat more calories than your body can use.

1 gram * of carbohydrate or protein gives		4 Calories
1 gram * of fat	gives	9 Calories

*(1 dime weighs 2 grams)

What is a *calorie* anyway? **A calorie is a measure of how much energy is stored in food.** This energy is released as heat when a food is burned. Scientists measure the number of calories in foods by burning each food under a container of water. The energy that is given off by the burning food heats up the water. This added heat is then measured to determine the number of calories.

One Calorie of energy will raise the temperature of one liter of water (about a quart) by 1° Celsius. One peanut contains about 6 Calories. This means that one peanut will raise the temperature of one liter of water by 6° Celsius when it is burned.

You burn food in your body, too, to get the energy you need to live. But your body does a slow "burn" so that the heat doesn't get released all at once and destroy your cells.

Some carbohydrate foods give you lots of "empty calories." These are foods like soft drinks and candy bars which

contain sugars and few or no other nutrients. These "empty
calorie" foods may crowd out your appetite for other more
nutritious foods that contain nutrients like vitamins and minerals as well as calories. One two-ounce candy bar has about as
much sugar as three pounds of apples. One twelve-ounce glass
of cola contains nine teaspoons of sugar, a lot of water, caffeine, some fizz, and no other nutrients.

The carbohydrate sucrose, plain old table sugar, is a cul-
prit of tooth decay as well. Sucrose is the favorite carbohydrate
of the *bacteria* that live in your mouth. They eat the sugar and
turn it into acids that destroy the enamel of your teeth. The
longer the acid stays on your teeth, the greater the damage
until, eventually, a cavity will form. That's why sticky, sugary
foods like chewy candy and dried fruits like raisins are the
hardest on teeth. **It's important to brush or rinse sticky foods
off your teeth right after you eat them.**

Calorie Chart

Food	Amount	Calories
Celery	1 stalk	5
Dill pickle	1	10
Carrot	1	20
Tomato	1	40
Green peas	1/2 cup	60
Apple	1	70
White bread	1 slice	70
Baked potato	1	90
Non-fat milk	1 cup	90
Peanut butter	1 tablespoon	95
Banana	1	100
Butter	1 tablespoon	100
Potato chips	10 chips	115
Whole milk	1 cup	160
Chocolate, candy	1 bar	240
Ice cream	1 cup	255
Hamburger on bun	1	350
Roasted peanuts (without shells)	1/2 cup	420

Which foods do you think contain fats?

Compare the number of calories for whole milk and non-fat milk; for baked potatoes and potato chips.

Calorie Counting

You can burn a peanut to get an idea of how much energy is stored within a food. Make sure there is an adult around when you do this experiment.

1. Stick the dull end of a needle into a cork so that the needle point is straight up.

2. Carefully stick a peanut (without the shell) onto the sharp end of the needle.

3. Place the cork and peanut on the base of a ring stand.

4. Pour one liter of water (a little more than a quart) into a shallow saucepan, or use a quart of water in a large juice can.

5. Record the water temperature with a thermometer that has a Celsius scale.

6. Place the saucepan or can on the ring stand, just above the peanut.

7. Light the peanut with a match. This will start the release of energy from the peanut.

8. Record the temperature of the water immediately after the peanut burns out.

9. Subtract your first water temperature reading (before burning) from your second reading (after burning). The difference will be equal to the amount of energy (Calories) released by the peanut. (Some heat will be lost to the ring stand and the air and will not be measured. This means that your Calorie count will be slightly lower than the actual number of Calories a peanut contains.)

How many Calories did your peanut contain?

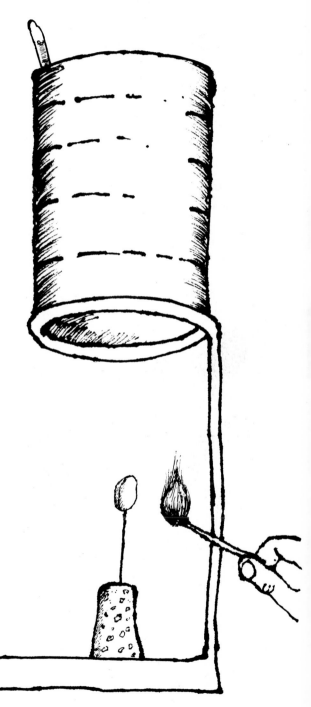

The Fats of Life

FAT FOOD SOURCES

<u>Plants</u>
Oils: corn
 cottonseed
 safflower
 peanut
 olive
Nuts
Grains
Legumes

<u>Animals</u>
Meat
Chicken
Fish
Egg yolks
Dairy products:
 cheese
 milk
 butter
 ice cream

Fats are another important energy nutrient. Because they contain more than twice as much energy as the same amount of protein or carbohydrate, they are the body's energy bank — a concentrated way of storing extra energy. That extra fat can come from too many carbohydrate, fat, or protein calories.

The layer of body fat beneath your skin insulates your body, and the fat around your organs cushions you as well. Think about that the next time you ride your bike over a rough spot and bounce around on your seat.

Fats add flavor to foods and carry some vitamins too. Foods with fats sit in your stomach longer than other kinds of foods. This means that meals with fats will keep you from feeling hungry longer than meals without fats.

Fats in animal foods are usually solid at room temperature — like the whitish fat of a steak or the yellowish fat of chicken. Vegetable fats are usually liquid at room temperature — like the corn oil your family may use in cooking. Margarine is a vegetable oil that is solid at room temperature. That's because margarine has been changed by a hardening process called *hydrogenation.* You may find the words "hydrogenated vegetable oils" on many food package labels.

People who want to avoid heart trouble may be told to eat fewer *saturated* fats (the animal fats and hydrogenated vegetable oils) and to eat more *polyunsaturated* fats (the liquid vegetable oils). They can do this by eating less red meat and fewer whole milk products, and by eating more chicken, fish, grains, and legumes. Substituting vegetable oil for butter in cooking helps too. This is important because **people who eat a lot of saturated foods are more likely to get heart disease.**

There are two vegetable fats to beware of — coconut oil and palm oil. Even though they come from vegetables, they're high in saturated fat. If you read food package labels, you will find that coconut oil and palm oil are almost always used in crackers and cookies and non-dairy creamers.

Fats cannot always be seen in foods. You may have tested for and found "invisible" fats in nuts, seeds, and grains, and in dairy products like cheese, milk, yogurt, and ice cream. French fries, doughnuts, and potato chips are all fried in fat. Chocolate bars contain lots of fat too.

EAT MORE

Fish
Chicken
Grains
Legumes
Margarine

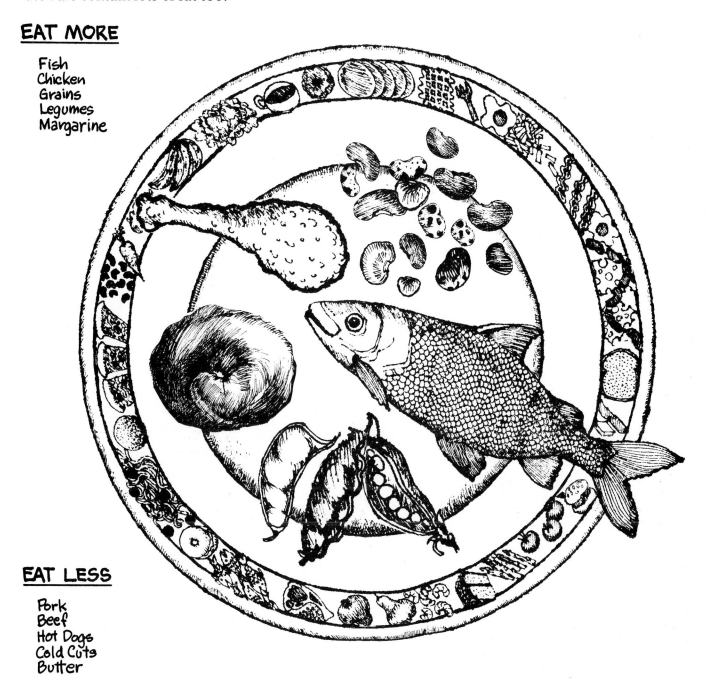

EAT LESS

Pork
Beef
Hot Dogs
Cold Cuts
Butter

Proteins — Putting It All Together

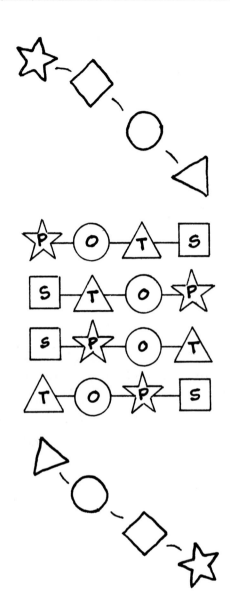

PROTEIN FOOD SOURCES

Plants
Grains
Legumes (dry peas and beans)
Nuts
Seeds

Animals
Fish
Chicken
Meat
Egg whites
Dairy products

Proteins are the important body-builder nutrients. They help your body grow and repair itself. They make up 3/4 of the solid matter of your body. Your skin, hair, bones, brain, and muscles are made of different proteins. So are the enzymes that control all your body processes from growth to digestion. Proteins are part of the red blood cells that carry oxygen around in your body. The *antibodies* in your bloodstream that fight off disease are proteins, too.

Your body can burn proteins for energy, but usually won't until you have met your body-building needs. Extra protein in your diet is burned for energy or goes into fat storage.

There are thousands of different kinds of proteins in plants and animals. What makes the thousands of proteins different?

Each protein is made up of building blocks called *amino acids* which are linked together in a chain. There are 20 kinds of amino acids that make up all proteins. **These 20 amino acids are arranged in different orders and in different amounts to produce the thousands of different proteins.** How can that be? Think of how many words can be made out of an alphabet with only 26 letters that are arranged in different combinations. Take the word "stop." Its four letters can spell the words "pots," "spot," "post," and "tops." The same four letters make five different words.

Your stomach and intestines take the proteins of foods and break them down into amino acid building blocks during digestion. Then the cells in your body rearrange the amino acids into your special kinds of proteins. Cow-type proteins are not the same as people-type proteins, although the same amino acids may be used to make each different protein combination.

Your body can make most of the amino acids it needs. But there are eight amino acids that it can't make for itself. **So you have to be sure to eat foods that contain these eight essential amino acids.** If any of these essential amino acids is missing from the protein in your diet, your body cannot grow or work as well.

Most animal foods contain all eight of the essential amino acids. That's why they are known as *complete protein* foods.

Plant foods like grains, seeds, and legumes (dry peas and beans) contain many of the eight essential amino acids, but each may be low in or missing one or two of them. So they are called *incomplete proteins.* **Plant foods are good sources of complete proteins when they are matched with certain other plant foods or dairy products.** The right protein combinations will contain a complete set of amino acids.

Grains and legumes together in a meal make a complete protein match. One tasty example of a protein match is peanut butter (legume) on bread (grain). See the "Protein Matches" box on this page for other food combinations.

People who eat only plant foods are called *vegetarians.* Some vegetarians eat milk and eggs as well. Many people in this country and around the world include vegetarian meals as a major part of their diets.

THE BEAN SCENE

Beans are important protein sources in many countries around the world. People in Japan and Brazil eat almost 50 pounds of beans per person each year. The average American eats only six pounds of beans a year.

Beans that stay on the vine until they are mature and dry are larger and contain less water than young green beans. That's why mature, dry beans have more protein than green beans. There is even more protein in bean seeds that are allowed to sprout. The sprouts of beans like mung beans are growing and they make more protein as they grow.

And when is a hamburger not a hamburger? When it's made of soybeans! Soybeans can be put into machines and shaped into long fibers that are woven into all kinds of meat look-alikes, including bacon, beef, chicken, and hamburger.

PROTEIN MATCHES

Grain + Legume
(peanut butter on whole wheat bread)

Grain + Milk food
(macaroni and cheese)

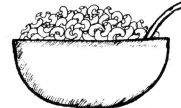

Legume + Seed
(hommos dip: chick peas and sesame seed paste)

LEGUME FAVORITES

There are different legume favorites in each part of the world:

India: chick peas
       lentils

Africa: cow peas
        lentils

Central
America: black beans

Mexico: kidney beans

Japan: soy beans
       mung beans

Water — You're All Wet

Most folks don't think of water as food. But water is another important nutrient. At least half of your body weight is water. If you weigh 80 pounds, 40 to 50 of them are water. Water helps dissolve the other nutrients so they can pass from your digestive tract into your bloodstream. Water is the liquid part of your blood. It carries wastes from your body and helps regulate your body temperature. **Every single process of your body depends on the presence of water.**

You can live for weeks without food, living off the fat of your body, but you can survive only a few days without water. Half of your body's water is lost and replaced every ten days. You need to consume huge amounts — some two to three quarts a day — to make up for the loss of water in urine and feces, and from breathing and *evaporation* from your skin.

Where does this water come from? You probably drink some of it straight from the tap, or in milk, juices, and soups. But much of your water comes from the foods you eat. Most fruits and vegetables are high in water. Leafy vegetables and fruits like watermelon are almost all water. Fish, eggs, and meat are at least half water. Even "dry" foods like bread and cereal contain a small amount of water. In three meals a day, even if you drink no beverages, you will take in nearly two pints of water.

A TOAST TO THE MORNING

1. Tomorrow morning, put your piece of hot toast on a cold surface for one minute.

2. Lift up the toast. What is on the table surface? Where did it come from?

Vitamin Alphabet Soup and Mineral Stew

Carbohydrates, fats, proteins, and water are nutrients that you consume in large quantities each day. Two other kinds of nutrients are vitamins and minerals. You need incredibly small amounts of them, but you can't live without them. The total amount of all vitamins needed in a day is 200 thousandths of a gram, about the weight of a pea. Some minerals like iodine are needed in the amount of millionths of a gram, an amount as tiny as a grain of sand.

Vitamins and minerals are the helper nutrients. They do many important jobs. They don't provide energy, but they act as enzyme helpers in the release of energy from the other nutrients. They also help speed up other chemical reactions that keep your body working. Every muscle you move, every sneeze you sneeze, depends on vitamins and minerals. So do the bones that hold you up and the teeth that chew your food.

Vitamins

Vitamins play important roles in the human body we didn't even know about until 80 years ago. For hundreds of years, people suffered from vitamin deficiency diseases (not enough of a vitamin) such as scurvy, beri-beri, and rickets, and didn't know the causes.

Vitamin C Goes to Sea

Sailors at sea on long voyages often fell ill with scurvy. Their muscles ached and their gums and flesh rotted. Their bones became brittle and their bodies were covered with bruises. They felt depressed and irritable, and many of them eventually died. Scurvy cost Vasco de Gama 100 out of his 160-man crew when he sailed around the Cape of Good Hope in 1498. Scurvy was the most common vitamin-deficiency disease in the world until the 18th century.

Some people realized that if they ate potatoes, cabbage, or citrus fruit (like limes and oranges), they wouldn't get the dread disease. The crews of all Spanish ships, including those of Columbus, were under orders to plant citrus trees. Each Spanish sailor heading for the Americas was given 100 orange seeds.

During the American Gold Rush of the 1840's, 10,000 Forty-Niners died of scurvy. Others escaped this fate by eating

a wild salad plant called "miner's lettuce" (winter purslane). And loggers in the backwoods of Maine learned to prevent scurvy by swallowing live black ants that had eaten pine needles.

What did all these foods have in common? They all contained vitamin C. But those folks didn't know that, because vitamin C wasn't even discovered until the 1920's.

What we know now is that **vitamin C (also called ascorbic acid) is needed to make a protein glue that holds your body cells together.** Without this protein, wounds don't heal and scurvy may take over. Dogs and cats can make their own vitamin C, thanks to their special kind of livers. In fact, everyone but guinea pigs, fruit bats, and people can make their own.

Since you can't make vitamin C with your liver, you need to take it in with your food every day. Citrus fruits, strawberries, tomatoes, spinach, and broccoli are all good sources of this nutrient.

We hear a lot about vitamin C, but there are at least fifteen other vitamins, including vitamins A, B, D, and K.

Does A Vitamin Save the Day?

Yes — **vitamin A is the vitamin which helps you see at night when the lights are dim.** It also helps keep your skin and inside body linings healthy and remodels your growing bones. You can get vitamin A from milk products and plant foods like carrot, squash, cantaloupe, sweet potato, spinach, and broccoli. Animal foods like liver actually contain vitamin A. Many plant foods contain an orange pigment, carotene, which your body has to *change* into vitamin A. Spinach and broccoli contain carotene but they don't look orange because their carotene is hidden by a dark green pigment.

B Vitamins — the Busy "B's"

The B vitamins are a group of nutrients that act as enzyme helpers to release energy from food. They help your body burn the fuel of carbohydrates, fats, and proteins. Niacin, thiamin, and riboflavin are three of the B vitamins you may have heard about on TV commercials or read about on food labels. These

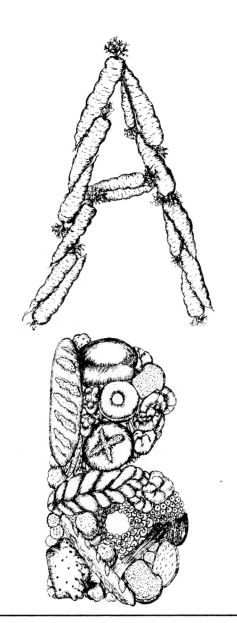

three vitamins are found naturally in whole grain products but are added to all enriched breads and cereals (that's why they're called "enriched"). Riboflavin is found in milk products as well.

Bone Up on Vitamin D

Vitamin D helps your bones absorb calcium. This so-called "sunshine vitamin" is made in your skin when sunlight hits it. You can also find it in milk. Most milk you drink has had vitamin D added — check the label to see. Cats and dogs get vitamin D when they lick body fat from the surface of their fur that has been exposed to sunlight.

Vitamin K — It's Blood Curdling

Do you know which vitamin helps your blood clot or coagulate? **It's vitamin K, the "Koagulations vitamin."** Most of the vitamin K is produced inside your intestinal tract by the billions of bacteria that live there. Other sources of this vitamin are spinach, broccoli, and milk. New-born babies often have a vitamin K deficiency because they are born with a sterile digestive tract (without any bacteria). As babies are born, they pick up bacteria from their mother and the surrounding environment. It takes a few days for these bacteria to make a home in the babies' intestines.

Vitamins on the Move

Vitamins A, D, and K are carried into your body in the fats of foods. The B vitamins and vitamin C are carried in the water of foods. The vitamins carried in water — B and C — are flushed from your body in urine when you have too much of them. So you need to eat foods with vitamins B and C every day. But the vitamins A, D, and K are carried in fats and are stored in your body's fat storage areas. This means that you don't have to eat them every day — you can store extras away in your liver and skin fat.

A diet with a variety of foods, including fruits and vegetables, will give you all the vitamins your body needs. People who take excess vitamins, usually as vitamin pills, can get too much of a vitamin. Too much of the kinds of vitamins that are stored in fats (A, D, and K) can poison your system.

LIVER LOVERS LOSE LAYERS

In January, 1969, some Dutch fishermen off the coast of Norway caught a huge halibut — some 6½ feet wide. Its liver, cooked in the ship's galley, made a feast for eleven of the twelve crew members (the twelfth hated liver). The men ate huge pieces of liver. Soon all eleven of them felt nauseated and headed for the side of the ship. They weren't seasick — they were suffering from overdoses of vitamin A.

The biggest eater had swallowed about 30 million units of vitamin A in his huge piece of liver (equal to about 2,000 vitamin tablets). The men's skin swelled up, turned red, and began to peel off in sheets. All the extra vitamin A had speeded up their skin production to many times the normal rate. That's the body's way of getting rid of vitamin A stored in the skin. Ten days later, when they reached home port, the men's skin was still peeling. Eventually, their vitamin A wore off, and they recovered. _____

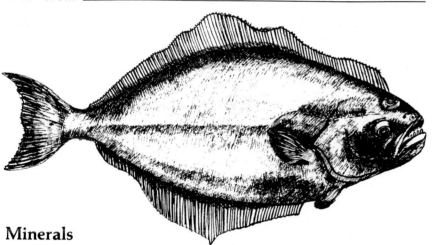

Minerals

Minerals like calcium, iron, sodium, fluoride, and zinc are important nutrients too. Besides being enzyme helpers, minerals do other jobs. *Calcium* helps build your bones and teeth. It also helps control your heartbeat and blood clotting. Every muscle you move depends on calcium.

Fluoride helps strengthen your teeth against decay. *Iron* helps the hemoglobin in your red blood cells carry the oxygen around in your bloodstream. "Iron-poor" blood can't carry as much oxygen and leaves you feeling tired.

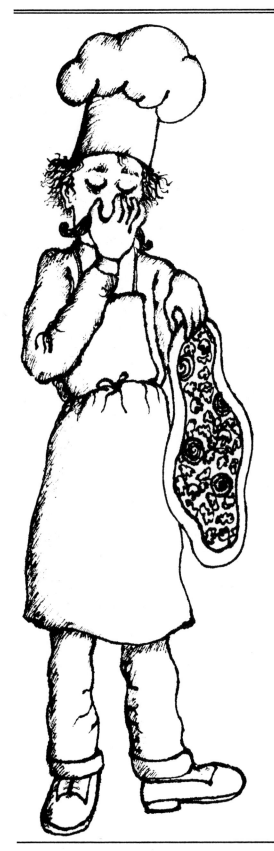

Milk, milk products, and dark green leafy vegetables are good sources of calcium. Fluoride may come from the water you drink or be supplied by your dentist or doctor. Iron can be found in liver, meat, poultry, fish, legumes, dark green leafy vegetables, and eggs. Most of the other essential minerals — sodium, zinc, copper, potassium, phosphorous, and magnesium — are widely available in many foods.

NOT AS EASY AS YOU "ZINC"

Rudy Coniglio says his trouble started on the night of July 27, 1969. Rudy ran a pizza shop in Closter, New Jersey. That night his cleaning help didn't show, so he had to clean up the shop by himself. He worked himself into exhaustion and came down with the flu. Rudy got some medicine from his family doctor and stayed home for a few days.

When he returned to work, he began making pizza dough. Then he started peeling tomatoes for the sauce. He tasted one tomato. It smelled and tasted rotten — like garbage! He went back into the kitchen to find some good tomatoes. Everything in the kitchen smelled rotten too — like the smell of burning plastic.

His restaurant workers came in, and they didn't smell anything strange. Rudy figured he was still sick, so he went home. He went outdoors to his backyard. The grass smelled too — twenty times stronger than the regular grass smell.

Rudy spent the next day sitting in the woods. He could stand the smell there. But he didn't eat any food because it tasted so bad. He went back to the doctor and got a new medicine. But that didn't help either. Rudy started living on cold milk, white grapes, and vanilla ice cream because they were the only foods that he couldn't taste.

He went from doctor to doctor. The ear, nose, and throat specialist sent him to a psychiatrist. Nothing helped. Rudy lost weight. All he could do was stand in the woods all day. All the doctors thought that Rudy's problem was in his head. It was, but he wasn't crazy.

By chance, he met Dr. Henkin, a specialist from the National Institutes of Health in Washington, D.C. Dr. Henkin told Rudy to open his mouth and stick out his tongue. Then he put a drop of something on it. Rudy couldn't taste anything. Dr. Henkin was pleased. "I know what you have and I can treat it," he said. Rudy couldn't believe it.

Dr. Henkin had discovered that Rudy had hypogeusia. Hypogeusia is a condition that makes a person lose the ability to distinguish different tastes. It usually distorts the senses of taste and smell as well. The drop Dr. Henkin had put on Rudy's tongue was hydrochloric acid (like stomach acid). To normal people it tastes very sour, but Rudy couldn't taste it at all.

Dr. Henkin did a series of tests on Rudy. He was especially interested in the amounts of the minerals copper and zinc that Rudy had in his blood and urine. He also did special tests on Rudy's taste buds. The tests showed that Rudy's body was low in zinc and copper and that his taste buds were abnormally worn down and frayed.

Dr. Henkin started Rudy on a supplement of a very small amount of zinc. Rudy's normal sense of taste started coming back by the end of the first week. By the end of the second week, things were even better. His taste buds looked normal again. Rudy went home and continued his zinc treatment. He was completely back to normal within a few months.

Later, Dr. Henkin discovered a zinc-containing protein in saliva which he called gustin. This gustin is what makes taste buds grow and work the way they should. Some people with hypogeusia have an abnormally low amount of this zinc-protein substance in their saliva. Finally, Rudy's mystery was solved.

What do you "zinc" of that? _____

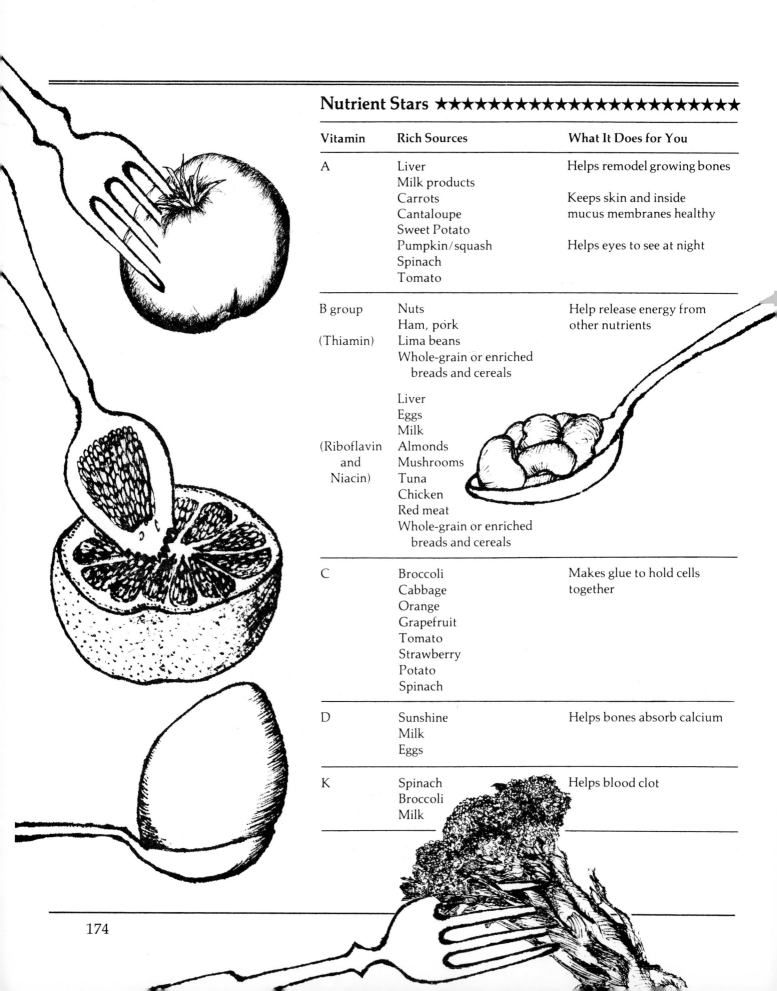

Nutrient Stars ★★★★★★★★★★★★★★★★★★★★★★★★★★★

Vitamin	Rich Sources	What It Does for You
A	Liver Milk products Carrots Cantaloupe Sweet Potato Pumpkin/squash Spinach Tomato	Helps remodel growing bones Keeps skin and inside mucus membranes healthy Helps eyes to see at night
B group (Thiamin)	Nuts Ham, pork Lima beans Whole-grain or enriched breads and cereals	Help release energy from other nutrients
(Riboflavin and Niacin)	Liver Eggs Milk Almonds Mushrooms Tuna Chicken Red meat Whole-grain or enriched breads and cereals	
C	Broccoli Cabbage Orange Grapefruit Tomato Strawberry Potato Spinach	Makes glue to hold cells together
D	Sunshine Milk Eggs	Helps bones absorb calcium
K	Spinach Broccoli Milk	Helps blood clot

Mineral	Rich Sources	What It Does for You
Calcium	Milk Cheese Yogurt Sardines Almonds Peanuts Spinach Broccoli	Makes bones and teeth Helps cement cells together Helps muscles to relax Helps blood clot
Iron	Liver Red meat Clams Almonds Walnuts Peas Beans Prunes Spinach	Carries oxygen in blood
Fluoride	Fluoridated water	Strengthens teeth against tooth decay
Zinc	Milk products Whole-grain breads and cereals Fruits Vegetables	Helps taste buds grow and work normally Part of many enzymes that help in body processes

Labels That Feed You a Story

Food labels can help you choose a diet that gives you the nutrients you need. They can't do the whole job, though, since many nutritious foods like fresh fruits and vegetables, fish, poultry, and eggs are not required by law to have labels.

Nutrition information is carried on the labels of many foods. This information is not required unless the food makes a nutritional claim like "low calorie," or has been enriched (had nutrients added). The nutrition labels, like the chili label on this page, will tell you the number of Calories per serving and the amounts of protein, carbohydrate, and fat. They also tell you how much of the recommended amount of eight nutrients the food contains. The percentage (%) of the Recommended Daily Allowance (called the U.S. RDA's) is only a general guide, not a perfect system for choosing food. Take a look around your kitchen. How many of the foods on your shelves have nutrition labels?

CHILI CON CARNE

Nutrition information per serving:

serving size = 1 cup
serving per container = 2
Calories 370   protein 18 G.
carbohydrate 24 G.   fat 22 G.

PERCENTAGE U.S. RECOMMENDED DAILY ALLOWANCES (U.S. RDA):

Protein	25	Thiamine	2
Vitamin A	50	Riboflavin	6
Vitamin C	4	Niacin	6
Calcium	6	Iron	15

Ingredients: water, beef, red beans, tomato paste, chili powder, garlic powder, spices, paprika, salt, artificial flavoring.

Net wt. 15 oz. (420 grams)

Besides nutrition information, you'll also find a list of ingredients on most labels. **The ingredients are listed in order of amount, from the most to the least.** So, if you see sugar listed first on your breakfast cereal label, that means that there's more sugar than any other ingredient.

The U.S. Food and Drug Administration (FDA) has set standards for some common foods. These standards require foods like ketchup, mayonnaise, and ice cream to contain certain ingredients. Since all ketchup contains the same basic ingredients, the manufacturers don't have to list them on the label.

Labels can be tricky. **Sugar comes in many different forms, so it is listed by many different names on labels.** You can find sugar, dextrose, sucrose, lactose, maltose, fructose, corn syrup, invert sugar, molasses, maple syrup, or honey listed on labels — they're all forms of sugar. Read labels and you'll be amazed to see how many foods contain sugar: ketchup, crackers, soups, salad dressings, and spaghetti sauce. Even some table salt has sugar (dextrose) added. Watch those labels!

SUGAR HAS MANY NAMES

Sugar
Dextrose
Sucrose
Lactose
Maltose
Fructose
Corn Syrup
Invert sugar
Molasses
Maple syrup
Honey

HOW SWEET IT IS!

For one day, pretend you are allergic to sugar. During that day you cannot eat any sugar.

Check your food labels carefully before you eat. Ask the person who cooked for the ingredients, if your food has already been prepared.

How difficult is it to be sugarless for one day?

How do you think people who are diabetic choose their foods?

Label Scavenger Hunt

Can you tell what foods these ingredient labels are describing? Which is the most nutritious food?

1. Sugar, modified food starch, cocoa processed with alkali, sodium phosphates (stabilizers), artificial flavoring, salt, sodium alginate (thickener), partially hydrogenated soybean and cottonseed oils, mono and diglycerides (emulsifiers), artificial flavoring.

2. Carbonated water, sugar, corn sweetener, natural flavoring, caramel color, phosphoric acid, caffeine.

3. Enriched egg noodles, salt, dehydrated chicken and chicken broth solids (BHA, propyl gallate and citric acid added to improve stability), natural flavorings, corn syrup, monosodium glutamate, hydrogenated vegetable oil, modified cornstarch, dehydrated onions, wheat starch, chicken fat, starch, potato starch, dehydrated parsley, flavoring and coloring.

4. Water, meat by-products, soybean meal, chicken parts, cracked pearled barley, ground soyhulls, iodized salt, potassium chloride, ethoxyquin (a preservative), sodium nitrite (for color retention), natural onion flavor, vitamin E supplement, zinc oxide, natural garlic flavor, vitamin A supplement, copper oxide, vitamin D_3 supplement, vitamin B_{12} supplement.

5. Sugar, lactose (milk sugar), corn syrup, artificial flavor, artificial color, processed with carbon dioxide.

(See page 210 for the answers.)

Allergies and Labels

Ingredient labels are especially important for people who have allergies to food. This means that their bodies are super-sensitive to certain foods. Some of the most common food allergies are to foods such as butter, cheese, eggs, milk, wheat, potatoes, nuts, fish, tomatoes, and mushrooms.

People have lots of different reactions to these foods. Some may have difficulty breathing or get an upset stomach or diarrhea. Others break out in hives or get headaches. Can you imagine trying to avoid all foods with milk or wheat flour in them?

On April 10, 1972, a ten-year-old boy in Dedham, Massachusetts, died when the opening of his windpipe swelled shut and choked him. This was an allergic reaction to the peanut butter in "Butterfinger" ice cream. The boy had known he was allergic to peanuts since he was three years old and had always avoided them. But this ice cream container gave no clue on its label that the ingredients included peanut butter.

This emphasizes the importance of having specific information on food labels. Many people have allergies that aren't quite as severe but can make them uncomfortable or very sick. Food manufacturers and the government need to make it easier for consumers to know what they are eating.

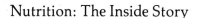

The Big Four

If labels aren't the whole story, how *can* you choose the foods that have what you need? The Four Food Groups are one answer. The Four Food Groups put similar foods together into categories. **Each category or group contains foods that are rich in the same nutrients.** These Four Food Groups are easy to recognize —

I. Fruits and Vegetables
II. Grains (breads and cereals)
III. Milk Products
IV. Beans, Nuts, Meat, and Eggs

Nutritionists have figured out how many servings of each food group you need for a balanced diet. If you eat the right number of servings from each of the four groups each day, you'll meet your nutrient needs. That makes choosing food a lot easier.

It's still not a perfect system. All foods within a group are not exactly the same. Foods within a group can vary in their nutrient values. **Some foods within a food group are better choices than others, since they give you the nutrients you need with the least sugar, salt, fat, or processing.** For example, milk and ice cream are in the same food group. Ice cream gives you the same kinds of nutrients as milk but fewer of them and lots more sugar and fat that add extra calories per cup.

Some foods are grouped into a fifth category called "Other" because they have few nutrients and offer little more than fat or sugar which add calories. The following chart will help you choose the best foods from each group.

Four Food Groups — Choices for Children

	Any Time	Sometimes	Now and Then
I. Fruits and Vegetables *Good sources of vitamins A and C, calcium and iron.* *You need 4 or more servings a day.*	Fresh fruits and vegetables Canned fruits (in own juices) Fruit juices (unsweetened) Vegetable juices	Canned fruits (in syrup) Fruit juices (sweetened) Canned vegetables (with salt) Dried fruits like raisins or apricots	French fried potatoes Olives Pickles Potato chips
II. Grain (Bread and Cereal) *Good sources of B vitamins, iron and protein.* *You need 4 or more servings a day.*	Whole grain bread and rolls Oatmeal Pasta (spaghetti, etc.) Rice Whole grain cereals (except granola)	Granola cereals (may be high in fat or sugar) White bread (enriched) Low sugar cereals	Highly sugared cereals
III. Milk Products *Good sources of protein, calcium, vitamins A and D, and riboflavin (B vitamin).* *You need 3 to 4 servings a day.*	Low-fat or skim milk Yogurt (plain) Cottage cheese (plain) Skim milk cheese Buttermilk	Yogurt (sweetened) Frozen yogurt Whole milk Hard cheeses (cheddar, muenster, Swiss, blue, brick)	Processed cheeses (American cheese, etc.) Ice cream Ice milk Cheesecake
IV. Beans, Nuts, Meat and Eggs *Good sources of protein, minerals (like iron) and B vitamins.* *You need 2 servings a day.*	Peanut butter Chicken or turkey (no skin) Fish (fresh or frozen) Shellfish Tuna (canned and drained) Dried peas and beans	Eggs Fish (canned, salted, pickled or smoked) Beefsteaks, roasts, stews or hamburger Ham, veal, pork or lamb Chicken or turkey (with skin)	Lunch meats (corned beef, ham, salami, liverwurst, etc.) Hot dogs Sausage Bacon
Other		Mayonnaise Salad oils Margarine	Butter / Cream cheese Cream / Sour cream Coconut or palm oil Packaged pastries Doughnuts Juice drinks Soft drinks Candy Deep fried foods

Any Time = any time you like   Sometimes = 2 to 3 times a week   Now and Then = once a week or less

An Apple a Day . . .

Look at one day of your meals — breakfast, lunch, dinner and snacks — to see if you're eating enough foods from each of the Four Food Groups.

1. Make a chart like the one below to keep track of your meals.

2. List the foods and number of servings you eat in each of the Four Food Group categories on your chart. The Four Food Groups Chart in this chapter can help you decide the correct categories.

3. Count up the number of servings you had in each food group for the whole day.

4. Did you eat enough servings in each food group to have a balanced diet for the day? In which groups are you low? How many foods did you have in the "Other" category?

Look at the Four Food Groups Chart for suggestions of foods you can eat to fill your food group needs.

	BREAKFAST	LUNCH	DINNER	SNACKS
I. FRUITS AND VEGETABLES	orange juice	pizza: tomato sauce green pepper		
II. GRAINS	corn flakes	pizza crust		
III. MILK PRODUCTS	milk	pizza cheese		
IV. BEANS, NUTS, MEAT & EGGS		pizza sausage		
V. OTHER	sugar			

Fruits and Vegetables

4 servings

Grains (bread and cereals)

4 servings

Milk Products

3 servings

Beans, Nuts, Meat and Eggs

2 servings

The Nutrient Disappearing Act

Watch carefully! Now you see it — now you don't. The nutrients in foods can disappear before they even reach your mouth. **The nutrient content of foods can be changed by the processing they go through between field and table, and by the way you store, prepare, and cook them.**

When wheat grains are ground into white flour, the bran and germ of the seed are removed. The bran and germ take with them many of the minerals and vitamins and some of the protein contained in the whole wheat kernel. Enriched white flour, which is used in most of the breads and crackers that Americans eat, has some of these nutrients put back into it. But not all the important nutrients can be or are put back in. So whole-grain products are more nutritious than those made of refined, enriched white flour.

KERNEL OF WHEAT

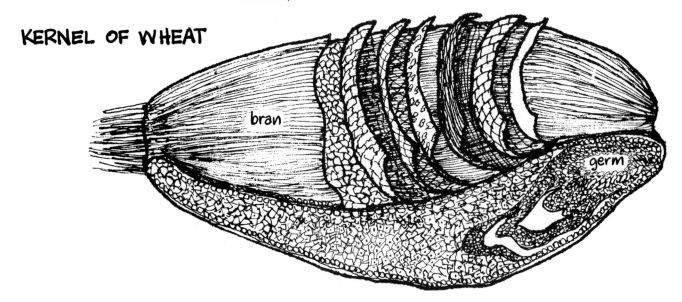

Cooking can easily destroy the vitamin content of foods, too. Since vitamins B and C are carried in the water of foods, they may easily drain out of foods into the cooking water. That's why it's more nutritious to eat vegetables that are slightly cooked or that have been steamed in a small amount of water. It's important to cover the pot in cooking, too, as vitamins may also escape in steam.

Vitamin C is also lost when fruits and vegetables are cut and exposed to the air and during the storage of foods in the refrigerator. After five days in the refrigerator, broccoli will have lost half of its vitamin C.

Dietary Guidelines: Changing the Food We "Chews"

CHOICES

1. Look at your everyday eating patterns by keeping a list of everything you eat in two days.

2. Try to follow the dietary goals for one week.

3. What kind of changes did you make in your food choices?

The Select Committee on Nutrition and Human Needs, a joint committee of the Department of Agriculture and the Department of Health and Human Services, has studied the eating habits of Americans to see how well we do at choosing the proper foods for our health and well-being. After hearing the testimony of dozens of experts, the committee recommended several dietary changes that affect both children and adults. The committee's dietary guidelines encourage us to:

- take in only as many calories in food as we use up in activities
- eat more fruits and vegetables and whole grains
- eat less refined sugar and fewer foods high in sugars
- eat less food that is high in fats:
    a. replace saturated animal fats with polyunsaturated plant fats
    b. eat less animal fat, eat more poultry and fish than beef and pork, which are high in saturated fat
- eat less salt and fewer foods high in salt

Think about these guidelines as you choose your meals and snacks.

Snack Choices

Anything you eat or drink any time of the day in between meals is a snack. The best snacks are foods you would also eat at meals. Choose snacks that don't give you just "empty calories" or more calories than you need. Here are some snack suggestions for you to choose from.

Best Bets

Fruits	Vegetables
fresh fruits	fresh vegetables
canned fruits	vegetable juices
(in their own juices)	
fruit juices (unsweetened)	
frozen fruit juice bars	
applesauce (unsweetened)	
cider	

Milk Products

milk (especially low-fat or
   skim)
yogurt (plain or with fresh
   fruit)
cottage cheese

Sandwiches

tuna
chicken
egg salad
peanut butter

Other

nuts and seeds (unsalted)
whole grain or enriched breads, rolls, bagels, etc.
peanut butter on celery, apples, etc.
cereal (unsweetened) and milk
water

Good Choices

Milk Products

cheeses
yogurt (sweetened)
frozen yogurt
chocolate milk
ice cream, ice milk, sherbet

Crackers and Cookies

cheese crackers
animal crackers
peanut butter crackers and
   cookies
graham crackers
oatmeal cookies

Dried Fruits

raisins
dates
apricots
prunes, etc.

Cakes

angel cake
applesauce, carrot and other
     fruit or vegetable cakes

Sandwiches

cheese
meat

Other

popcorn
nuts and seeds (salted)

O.K. Once in a While

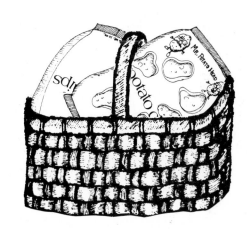

lunch meats, ham, hotdogs
potato chips, corn chips, salted pretzels, salty crackers
commercial pies, pastries, doughnuts
soft drinks and imitation fruit drinks
chocolate and other candy

BRUSH YOUR TEETH AFTER ANY SUGARY SNACK

Food Magic

ABRACADABRA

1. Name one food that gets softer when it's cooked, and one food that gets harder.

2. What food changes color or taste when it's cooked?

3. Explain what is happening in the foods to cause each of these changes.

Cooking magically changes foods before your eyes. Soft foods become hard and hard foods become soft. Cooking breaks down tough plant fibers so that plant foods become easier to digest. Some nutrients, like niacin, which are locked up in raw foods, are released when the food is heated. In foods like soybeans, cooking destroys a poisonous substance within, so the food becomes edible. Some nutrients like vitamin C may be destroyed by heat. Heat may change the color and taste of food as well.

Cheese

Cheese is a story of change. The cheese legend tells of an Arab who began a journey across the hot desert. Around noon he stopped to drink the milk he had stored in a dried calf stomach (one of the first canteens). He opened the calf stomach and was disappointed — the milk had changed to a curdy white substance floating in water. He was very hungry and thirsty, so he tasted this strange lumpy mixture anyway. It was delicious. (He was overheard to say, in amazement, "Jeez!")

There are at least 400 different cheeses available around the world today, but they all got their start in much the same way. Three things are needed to make a cheese — milk, heat, and an enzyme called rennin. Rennin is an enzyme people and other mammals have in their stomachs which helps digest milk. It curdles milk to form lumpy curds and liquidy whey. (Little Miss Muffet knew all about curds and whey.) The curds that contain most of the milk protein are then easier to digest.

The Arab in the desert had his milk stored in a calf stomach. The calf stomach probably still contained some of the rennin enzyme. The hot sun warmed the milk, which reacted with the rennin to form curds and whey.

Say Cheese! (A Whey-Out Recipe)

You can make your own cheese at home or in school. The ingredients are:

1 cup of milk
3 to 5 drops of liquid rennet (a kind of rennin)
Saucepan for milk
Hot plate or stove
Piece of cheesecloth

(You can usually find rennet at a supermarket or drugstore.)

1. Put the cup of milk into a pan and heat the milk to 88° F.
    Use a clean thermometer to measure the temperature —
    too much heat will destroy the cheese-making enzyme.

2. Add 3 to 5 drops of the liquid rennet enzyme to the warm
    milk.

3. Keep the milk at 80° F until it curdles — in about 12 to 18
    hours. You can keep the milk in a warm (lowest setting)
    oven overnight.

4. Pour the curds and whey from the pan into a cheesecloth
    held over a bowl. A rubber band may hold the cheesecloth
    open over the bowl. Collect the curds in the cheesecloth
    as the liquidy whey drains into the bowl.

In 15 to 20 minutes, the curd will become more solid and
will drain slowly. When the curd is almost solid, you can
squeeze out the rest of the whey.

Your cheese is ready for tasting. You may want to add a
little bit of salt for taste, or try it on a salted cracker.

Bread

Bread owes part of its rise in fame to proteins too. Wheat
flour contains a stringy protein called *gluten.* This protein
forms the skeleton of breads or cakes when it is baked. Yeasts
(microscopic plants) added to the dough feed on sugars and
starches. In a warm environment, the yeasts ferment (change)
these carbohydrates into alcohol and a gas called carbon dioxide. The carbon dioxide bubbles try to escape the sticky gluten.
As they push through the dough, they make the dough light
and porous, and the dough rises.

Egyptians are given credit for making the first baked
goods with rising dough. No one knows for sure how they discovered leavened bread. A good guess is that wild yeasts
dropped out of the air onto their dough, fed on its sugars, and
gave it gas. Corn flour and rye flour contain no gluten protein,
so they cannot rise to any occasion.

Start Loafing!

Try your hand at bread baking. There are lots of different bread recipes, but they all include the same basic combination of ingredients: flour, liquid, shortening, sweetener, and magical yeast.

Use this simple recipe first, and then you can experiment using different kinds of flours, water instead of milk, margarine or butter instead of oil, or honey or molasses instead of sugar.

You can add many different ingredients to make your bread taste the way you like it. Try adding onions, chives, grated cheese, or seeds like caraway, sesame, or poppy.

You will need:

1 cup water	Saucepan
1 cup milk	Large mixing bowl
6 tablespoons oil	Dishtowel
2 tablespoons sugar	Wooden spoon
2 teaspoons salt	Measuring cup and spoons
5½ to 6 cups flour	2 bread pans
1 package (or 1 tablespoon) active dry yeast	Oven

Putting ingredients together

1. Add milk, water, and oil to the saucepan. Heat at a low temperature until lukewarm (105 to 115° F. It will feel warm but not hot on your wrist). The yeast needs a warm liquid in order to work its magic. It will die if it's too hot.

2. Pour this warm liquid into a mixing bowl. Add the yeast and stir until it dissolves.

3. Add sugar, salt, and 2 cups of flour. Beat vigorously (100 strokes by hand).

4. Add the rest of the flour (3½ cups) and stir well. Your dough should pull away from the sides of your bowl. It will be very sticky.

Kneading

1. Measure 1/2 cup of flour.

2. Dust the table or breadboard surface lightly with some of this flour, and flour your hands. Keep the rest of the flour aside to work into the dough as needed.

3. Put the dough on the table and knead it for 6 to 8 minutes until the dough is shiny and elastic.

Kneading means pushing down on dough with the heels of your hands and then folding the other edge of the dough back onto itself towards you. Then push down into the dough again. Turn the dough a quarter turn around after each push so that all the dough gets kneaded. This gentle stretching of the sticky gluten in dough is important for making your dough light and airy.

Setting Dough to Rise

1. Put the ball of dough in a large, lightly-oiled mixing bowl. Turn the dough around in the bowl to oil its surface.

2. Cover the bowl with a clean towel. Place the bowl in a warm place until it rises to double its size (about one hour).

Punching Down and Making Loaves

1. Gently punch the dough with your fists. This will get out large air pockets which would make large holes in the bread.

2. Divide the dough in half. Shape it into two loaves, rolls, or any shape you want.

3. Place the dough into two greased bread pans.

4. Allow it to rise again until it has almost doubled in size.

Baking

1. Bake in a pre-heated oven at 375° F. for 45 minutes. The bread is done when the loaf shrinks away from the sides of the pan and sounds hollow when tapped.

2. Take the loaves from the pans and cool on a rack.

There are other leavening agents besides yeast which help breads and cakes to rise. Air beaten into a batter will expand during baking. Eggs are good leavening agents, too, as they take in a lot of air when beaten. Baking soda and baking powder each react to form carbon dioxide bubbles within an up-and-coming batter.

What Puts the Pop in Popcorn?

No matter how dry seeds may seem to be, they all contain a small amount of water that keeps them alive until sprouting time. This little bit of water is what brings you popcorn.

When a kernel of popping corn is heated quickly, the water inside boils to become a steamy gas that explodes the tough seed coat. As the gas bursts free, it expands quickly, puffing up the soft inner part of the seed.

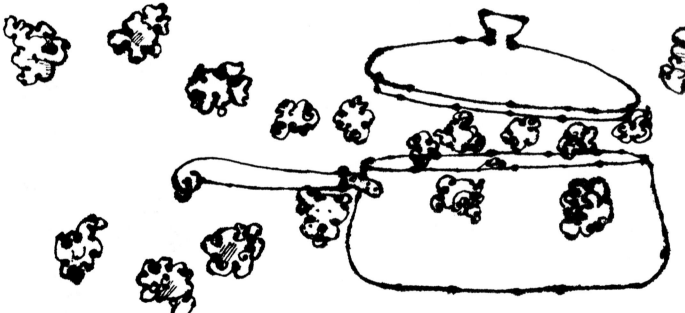

Popcorn Poppability

The way corn pops depends on how much moisture the seeds have. Here's a way to see this in action. You will need:

A pot with a cover	6″ ruler
Fresh popcorn kernels	Cooking oil
Two cookie trays	Oven
A measuring cup	

Directions

1. Preheat your oven to 200° F.

2. Measure 1/4 cup of popcorn kernels.

3. Spread the corn in a thin layer on a cookie sheet.

4. Heat the corn in the oven for 1½ hours.

5. Meanwhile, measure another 1/4 cup of popcorn kernels.

6. Put 3 tablespoons of cooking oil in the bottom of your popcorn pot. Add the 1/4 cup of popcorn.

7. Heat the popcorn and oil over high heat. Once the popping begins, cover and shake until the popping stops.

8. Pour the popcorn out of the pan onto another cookie sheet or paper toweling.

9. Count the number of unpopped kernels.

10. Measure the 10 largest popped kernels and list the numbers on a piece of paper.

11. Add the numbers and average them.

12. At the end of the 1½ hours, take the other popcorn kernels out of the oven.

13. When the corn kernels have cooled, pop them in 3 tablespoons of oil in the same way you popped the first batch.

14. Count the number of unpopped kernels in this batch.

15. Measure the 10 largest popped kernels and list the numbers.

16. Add the numbers and average them.

   - How do the two average sizes of largest popped kernels compare?
   - What did heating the corn in the oven do to it?
   - What other variations of this experiment can you think of?

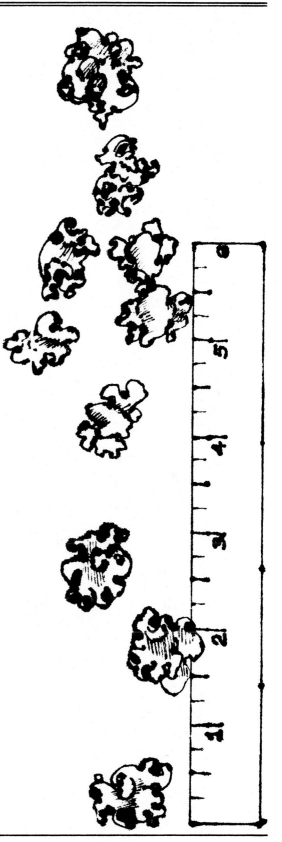

It's an Inside Job

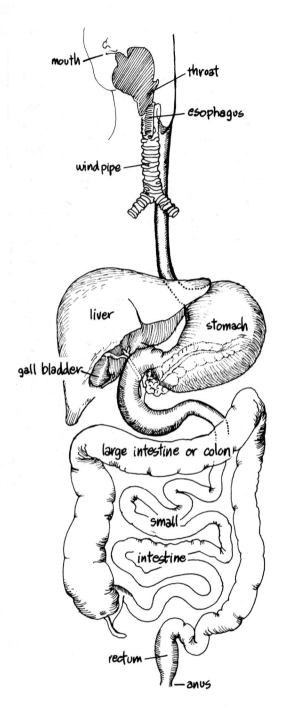

mouth

throat

esophagus

wind pipe

liver

stomach

gall bladder

large intestine or colon

small

intestine

rectum

anus

TRAVELING TIMES

Mouth (1 to 2 minutes)
Esophagus (4 to 6 seconds)
Stomach (1 to 6 hours)
Small Intestine (2 to 9 hours)
Large Intestine (1 to 3 days)

Some of the biggest changes in food happen inside of you. The food you eat contains carbohydrate, fat, and protein — nutrients that are too big to be absorbed and used by your body. These nutrients have to be digested (broken down) into smaller building blocks before you can even take them into your bloodstream.

The 32-foot digestive tract that runs through your body does this trick. The digestive tract is a muscular tube that keeps the food moving along (usually in one direction) as it's being digested. The muscles push the food along the way that you push toothpaste out of a tube, by pressing the tube together right behind the food that's moving through.

At different places along the digestive tract, enzymes are dumped in to digest the large nutrients into smaller building blocks that can be absorbed into the bloodstream. Your blood then does the job of carrying these building blocks around to feed all your millions of cells.

Food travels from your mouth to your esophagus, on to your stomach, and then to your small intestine. Whatever food has not been digested then passes into your large intestine and out the anus. This entire trip usually takes a day and a half.

Can You Swallow This?

Digestion usually begins in your mouth. When you chew, your teeth grind, tear, and mash foods into smaller pieces. Small pieces of food can be digested by enzymes more easily than large ones. At the sight of food, you may begin to drool. Your saliva contains the enzyme amylase that breaks starch down into sugars.

Your saliva also moistens the food so it can easily slide down your throat. Your salivary glands make at least a quart of this juice every day. Your tongue is the muscle that pushes the food on its way. It is also your taster. It's covered with 9,000 taste buds that help make eating a sensory treat. Scientists have discovered that our sense of taste is at its best two times a day — around 5 to 7 p.m. and 3 a.m. So a middle-of-the-night snack might taste pretty good if you're up for it.

SPIT-SPLIT

1. Take a starchy unsalted cracker or a raw piece of potato.

2. Chew it and keep it in your mouth for a few minutes until it begins to taste sweet.

3. What is happening here?

Tongue Twisters

Q-Tip Dip

Your tongue can select four tastes — sweet, sour, bitter, and salty. Most foods are a combination of these four tastes.

You can use different tasting solutions to find out where each of the four tastes is located on your tongue.

You will need: sugar water, salt water, lemon juice (sour), quinine water (bitter), and at least four different Q-tips (or cotton balls).

1. Dip a Q-tip into the sugar water solution. Rub it on your tongue, one spot at a time, until you have covered the whole tongue. On a tongue drawing, mark the area where you tasted the sugar water.

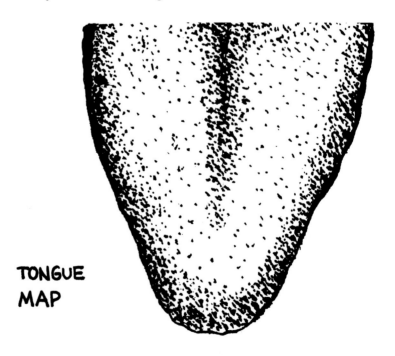

TONGUE MAP

2. Rinse your mouth with water between tests.

3. Repeat the test with the salt water, lemon juice, and quinine water. Use different colors to mark the different tastes on the tongue map.

ARE YOUR TASTE BUDS DUDS?

Try tasting five different foods and check which of the four tastes you detect in each food. Make a chart like the one below:

	Sweet	Salty	Bitter	Sour
1. cheese		x		
2.				
3.				
4.				
5.				

Come to Your Senses

Are your senses of taste and smell connected? Get a friend to help you. Have the friend blindfold you. Hold your nose, taste the food your friend gives you, and see if you can guess what it is.

Dry It!

Have you ever tried tasting with a dry tongue? Wash out your mouth with water and dry off your tongue with a tissue. Now close your eyes and try tasting a food that a friend gives you. Can you guess what it is? Wet your tongue and try again.

When you swallow your food, it takes four to eight seconds for it to travel down the esophagus tube to your stomach. A flap closes over your windpipe as you swallow to keep food from heading towards your lungs. If you've ever had a food go "down the wrong pipe," you were probably inhaling while you were eating, and your flap didn't close in time.

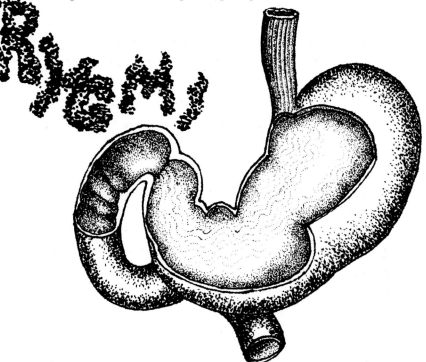

The stomach is a hollow pear-shaped muscle about the size of your two fists. When you eat, it expands to become even larger. Adult stomachs are eight inches from top to bottom and four inches across. They can stretch to be twice as long — 16 inches — when full. Your stomach has rings of muscles at each end to regulate the coming and going of food.

The stomach is lined with glands that go into action every three or four hours whether food is present or not. Just thinking about food can start your stomach glands giving off digestive juices that gurgle and rumble as your empty stomach churns away. The fancy name for stomach and intestine rumbles is "borborygmi." Try that one out on your friends!

The stomach's digestive juices are made of water, hydrochloric acid, and an enzyme that breaks down proteins. Your stomach makes 2 to 2½ quarts of juices daily. The acid in these gastric juices activates the enzyme and helps to break down the protein as well. The acid kills some of the bacteria you swallow with your food.

Why doesn't this stomach acid digest the wall of the stomach itself? Fortunately there is a layer of *mucus* that lines and protects the inside of the stomach. When you're nervous, you

may produce more stomach acid. Some people produce extra acid and don't seem to have as much of a protective layer as others. Their stomach acid may burn a small hole called an *ulcer* in their stomach lining. No one is really sure why some people get ulcers and others don't.

Heartburn comes from partially digested food backing up the esophagus. The acid of your digestive juices tastes sour and burns on the way up. *Vomiting* is an even more violent reversal of the muscle's action. It may happen when you're nervous, when you eat food or drink that irritates your stomach, or when you're sick with a virus. The force of vomiting comes mostly from the diaphragm muscles that help in breathing and not from the stomach itself.

The average meal churns around in your stomach for three to five hours, though some foods may hang around longer. Fats in foods slow down the stomach's action so that food is digested more slowly and sugar enters the bloodstream at a steady rate. That's why foods with fats keep you feeling full longer than pure carbohydrate or protein meals. Your stomach is affected by your mood, too. If you're sad, it takes longer to digest your food than if you're happy.

When you swallow your food, you swallow air too. Swallowed air causes most of the gas in your stomach and intestinal tract. One way of getting rid of that gas is to burp, but, please, not at the table unless you live in a country where that's acceptable. In some countries it's actually considered good manners to burp at the end of a meal. That tells the cook you enjoyed the meal.

SEE-THROUGH STOMACH

Much of what we know about the stomach's action is based on observations that a U.S. Army doctor, Dr. Beaumont, made back in 1822. That year a young French-Canadian trapper named Alexis St. Martin was accidentally shot in his left side with a load of buckshot. He was working on Mackinac Island in the straits between Lake Michigan and Lake Huron where Dr. Beaumont was stationed.

Beaumont saved Alexis St. Martin's life but was unable to close the wound completely. St. Martin was left with a hole in his belly leading into his stomach. Beaumont was able to use this window into St. Martin's stomach to study the stomach's activity. He would tie different kinds of foods to strings, lower them into the stomach, and then take notes on the effect of the juices on each of the different foods. He could also see how the stomach worked when its owner was angry or afraid.

Beaumont published a book on his observations that is still read today. And even with a hole in his belly, Alexis St. Martin lived to the age of 83! _____

The stomach's churning and chemical reactions slowly change solid food into a thick soupy mixture. The ring of muscles at the lower end of the stomach gives the "go-ahead," and the soupy mixture enters the small intestine in a series of small, spoon-sized squirts.

The small intestine isn't really very small at all. It is a tube 22 feet (seven meters) long (four to five times taller than you are), where most of your food's digestion takes place. It takes your food from two to nine hours to move all the way through. **The small intestine adds more enzymes to break down the fats, proteins, and carbohydrates.** The pancreas contributes some enzymes too, and the liver and gall bladder add bile that helps break down fats. All these chemicals slowly digest the digestible food into building blocks. **Then the finger-like projections in the lining of the small intestine absorb these building blocks into your bloodstream.**

Gas, Alas — This Too Shall Pass

Millions of bacteria call the intestines home. Some of these bacteria give you gas. Baked beans are believed to contain two sugars that you have no enzymes for. These two sugars, stachyose and raffinose, can't be digested in the upper part of the small intestine. When they move into the lower part of the intestine, bacteria feed on these sugars to produce gases of carbon dioxide, hydrogen, and methane. These gases make you feel uncomfortable, and some eventually escape. Gas (*flatus* is the fancy word) is not usually expelled until three to seven hours after you eat the beans. So, if you time it right,

you may be able to enjoy your beans after all.

Not all beans are equal. Some produce less gas than others. There have been efforts made to breed a gasless bean, but they haven't been successful as yet.

Beans are not the only offenders. Other gassy foods are cabbage, broccoli, brussel sprouts, and cauliflower. Some folks avoid melon and onions too.

A California scientist reports that most of the bean's gas-producing sugars can be eliminated. You can do this by boiling the beans in lots of water for 10 minutes, then soaking them overnight, and replacing the water with fresh water before they are cooked.

"Breaking wind" (as it was known in the Middle Ages) has never been acceptable at the table. The Chinese and Indians were forbidden this kind of relief as early as the 6th century B.C. The Roman emperor Claudius considered a law to legalize "breaking wind" at the table when he heard of a modest man who had endangered his health trying to keep from passing gas.

The U.S. Department of Agriculture developed a system, while studying suitable food for astronauts, for measuring the "flatus-producing effect" of different foods. That's important information for astronauts who orbit for days in a small space capsule.

Some adults do not produce the enzyme necessary to break down the milk sugar, lactose. It is here in the large intestine that the bacteria ferment milk sugar to produce acids and gases that give cramps and diarrhea. Most people with "lactose intolerance" can drink a single glass of milk without getting these symptoms. But their digestive tracts can more easily handle soured or fermented milk products like cheese, yogurt, and sour cream because the lactose has already been partially digested by fermentation.

Getting to the End

You are not able to digest and absorb all that you eat. Digestive tracts of different animals vary in this ability. Mice

BEAN GAS MILEAGE

Not all beans are equal. Some produce less gas than others.

Least gas: black-eyed peas
lima beans
garbanzo beans

Middle gas: green peas
small white beans
pinto beans

Most gas: soy beans
black beans
pink beans

are able to use almost all they eat, while grasshoppers can use less than 1/3 of the grass they consume. Elephants have a notoriously poor digestive tract. A 13,000-pound elephant has to eat 780 pounds of vegetation a day because most of this food just passes on through.

Your digestive tract is certainly better than an elephant's, but it depends on what you eat as to how well you do. Vegetable foods are more difficult to digest than animal foods because of the tough cellulose *fibers* of plants. But fiber from vegetables, fruits, and grains is very important for your health. You need fiber in your diet because it provides bulk that helps move waste and bacteria out of your body.

The undigested wastes pass out of your small intestine into your large intestine. This five-foot tube is much shorter than the small intestine, but it has a wider opening which gives the larger intestine its name. **The large intestine (also known as the colon) is where water from the digestive juices gets reabsorbed back into the body.** It is also the place where feces (from the Latin, *faeces,* for dregs) are stored until it's time to go.

Normal feces are made mostly of water. The solid part is from 1/3 to 1/2 bacteria (most of which are dead). The rest is undigested food such as plant fibers, fruit skins, seeds, and the old linings of the digestive tract. These vegetable fibers give the bulk that helps move the feces along. Feces are held in the rectum by muscles until the spirit (muscle action) moves you and you have the time to go.

Bowel movements usually expel the feces within 36 to 48 hours after you eat. What you don't digest of your Sunday dinner will leave sometime Tuesday. For some folks, it will leave on Monday and for others not until Wednesday or Thursday. There's no law that says you have to move your bowels once a day. That's a common pattern, but for some people the urge comes only every two or three days.

Many Americans seem to watch their bowels as much as they watch TV. U.S. bowel watchers spend more than $100 million a year for laxatives that keep them on the go. Many of these remedies are unnecessary interruptions. **Most doctors just recommend foods with a lot of fiber and plenty of exercise for**

encouraging your bowel reflex.

Sometimes you may get the urge to go at an inconvenient
time, or you may be nervous and hold back too long. When
this happens, more water is absorbed back into the body as the
feces stay in the rectum longer. Feces may get hard and dry and
be harder to move along. That's called *constipation*.

At other times you may be nervous, have an infection or
have eaten some food that disagrees with you. Then your large
intestine tries to push the food along too fast. The feces don't
stay in the colon long enough for the body to reabsorb the water.
That's known as *diarrhea*.

Your Plate Can "Weight"

Being fat was once a sign of wealth and status in most societies. Even today it is fashionable in some countries. But most people now recognize that being fat or even overweight can be dangerous to their health. **Being overweight puts a strain on your body and makes you more likely to suffer from diabetes, arthritis, high blood pressure, and kidney and heart disease.**

And excess fat that some people put on as young children can stay with them for life. All infants produce special fat cells to store fat. When babies gain too much weight, these fat cells can triple or quadruple in number and never be lost again. That doesn't mean that fat babies will always be fat, they may just have to work harder not to be. Being fat is no fun either. Studies have shown that overweight people are often treated unfairly by others who judge them by weight alone.

What is "overweight?" "Ideal" weight and height tables have been developed by insurance companies based on the average weights of thousands of people through the years. Insurance companies know that a person is a worse health risk if she/he weighs even ten pounds more than average. In these tables, ideal weights are given for different heights and different frame sizes. People with larger skeletons can hold more weight. But weight-height tables are not perfect guides.

A person is considered overweight if she/he weighs more than 10 percent above the ideal weight for her/his height and frame size. *Obesity* is something else. It means that a person has an excess accumulation of fat. Young men are made up of about 1/8 fat, and young women are about 1/5 fat. The rest of the body is muscle, bone, blood and other tissues. Obesity means going over these fat limits. Because extra fat is stored under the skin, lifting a fold of skin and measuring its thickness is one way of telling if a person is "overfat."

A person can be overweight and not be obese, if the extra weight comes from muscle instead of fat. Remember, muscle tissue weighs more than fat tissue. An athlete or dancer with well-developed muscles may weigh more than the "ideal" weight on the charts without being "overfat."

Many Americans are overweight. The American Seating Company says that American bottoms have expanded nearly two inches in the last thirty years! That's why the seats at new football stadiums are wider than those in older ball parks.

Why are so many Americans overweight? One reason is that we often eat when we don't even feel hungry. There are lots of reasons why we overeat. Sometimes we overeat when we are nervous, bored, or unhappy. At other times we overeat to please our parents or because food is offered to us as a reward. Some folks are famous for being overeaters, and they may have another excuse. King Louis XIV is one of them.

THE ROYAL FLUSH

King Louis XIV ruled in France from 1643 to 1715. He had an incredible appetite. King Louis always ate about twenty different dishes at a meal. Usually he ate three soups, five main courses, three fowls, and two fish and vegetable dishes. He would taste a few roasts, then a few shellfish, a few more vegetable dishes, then nibble at some desserts and finish up with a few hard-boiled eggs. With his personal income of $10 million a year, he could afford the food bill.

King Louis usually ate alone in his bedroom, but when he dined in public, people would drive out from Paris and line up to file past him. His eating was the evening's entertainment.

King Louis' teeth rotted and were pulled out by the time he was 40. He still ate. When he finally died, his autopsy revealed intestines that were twice as long as the average man's — some 50 feet long — and contained one very oversized tapeworm.

The tapeworm that lived in King Louis' intestines shared his meals with him. (The tapeworm is a long, flat worm that lives in the small intestines of animals. It doesn't have its own digestive tract, so it depends on those of other animals to do the job for it.) That's why King Louis could eat so much without becoming enormous. Tapeworms in people are pretty rare these days because of careful handling of food. So if you eat huge amounts of food, you probably can't blame a tapeworm!

FATTER FANNIES

1960

1970

1980

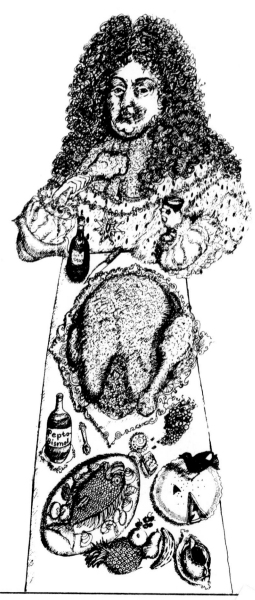

Energy In — Energy Out

What does it take to keep your weight steady? All you need to do is balance the number of calories you eat with the number of calories you use up in your daily activities. **If the number of calories you take in is equal to the number of calories you burn up, your weight will stay the same.**

The number of calories you need depends on your size, weight, age, rate of growth, body chemistry, and level of activity. Most girls and boys between the ages of 10 and 14 need a daily intake of from 2,400 to 2,800 Calories. Older boys require more calories than any other age group. When you are young, and your body is still growing, you need more calories than when you become full grown.

Three thousand five hundred Calories equal one pound of body fat. It doesn't matter whether those calories come from carbohydrates, fats, or proteins. For every extra 3,500 Calories you take in that you don't burn up, you will gain one pound of fat. And for every 3,500 Calories that you burn up, over the amount you eat, you will lose one pound of fat. If you eat just 100 extra Calories a day (two cookies), you may put on one pound a month and over ten pounds a year!

Most people who count calories pay attention only to the incoming calories. But outgoing calories used in activity count too. A one-mile walk (60 Calories' worth) can cancel out a small piece of fudge, one cup of spaghetti, or a California navel orange.

A hamburger is about a 40-minute jog, a 60-minute bike ride, or 289 minutes of just sitting around. Take a look at the chart on the opposite page. About how long would it take you to work off some of your other favorite foods? (Remember that the more you weigh, the more calories you use up on any activity.)

Some people's daily work requires greater than average inputs of energy. Lumberjacks in northern Minnesota years ago used to eat 9,000 Calories a day and not get fat. Chopping trees and hauling them out of the woods used up great amounts of energy.

Most of us don't get that much exercise these days. Our daily lifestyle is much less active because of machines that do the work for us. Today we use machines like the telephone and let our fingers do the walking instead of our legs.

Calorie-Exercise Equivalents

	Food	Amount	Calories	Number of Minutes Required to Work Off				
				Sitting	Walking	Biking	Swimming	Jogging
Main Dishes	Fried egg	1	110	85	21	13	10	5
	Tuna fish sandwich	1	273	208	53	34	25	14
	Peanut butter and jelly sandwich	1	290	223	55	35	26	15
	Hamburger on bun	1	350	270	67	42	32	18
	Pizza	1 slice	185	142	36	23	17	9
	Spaghetti and meatballs	2 cups	354	273	68	43	32	18
	Haddock or similar fish	1 piece	71	55	14	9	6	4
Fruits and Vegetables	Carrot	1	42	32	8	5	4	2
	Potato, boiled or baked	1	100	77	19	12	9	5
	Green beans	½ cup	15	15	3	2	1	3/4
	Apple	1 medium	80	65	16	9	7	4
	Strawberries	10	37	29	7	6	4	3
	Orange	1	63	52	13	8	6	4
	Orange juice	8-ounce glass	120	92	23	15	11	6
Other Common Snacks	Doughnut	1	150	116	29	18	13	8
	Peanuts	20	120	92	23	15	11	6
	Popcorn without butter or margarine	1 cup	25	20	5	4	3	2
	Potato chips	15	172	130	34	21	16	9
	Ice cream	1 cup	270	210	54	32	24	14
	Soda	1 can, 12 ounces	155	123	32	20	15	8
	Chocolate chip cookies	2 medium	100	77	19	12	9	5

Epilogue

Well, that's the story. At least, it's the beginning. The rest is up to you.

You've learned fitness boosts and games to give your lifestyle a lift. You know how to find your pulse to keep track of how hard you work. You've met the muscles that help you move. You know how to get stronger, last longer, and S-T-R-E-T-C-H.

You've seen how smoking and stress can slow you down. You've learned how relaxercisers and deep breathing can pick you up.

And you've learned how you wear your food. You can rate your plate for the nutrients it contains. You've met plant travelers, and animal protein machines. You can read a label, tickle your taste buds, make cheese, bake bread, plant a garden, see through commercials, and see life from a food's point of view.

That's a lot of inside information. How can you make it work for you? **Choices are the key.** Do as you see fit. Physically fit. Not just for now, but for life.

Answer Key

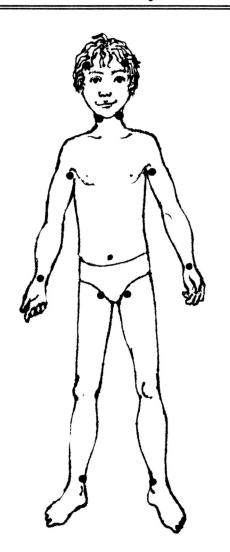

Page	Answer
25	Muscle Riddle: They both have the same number of muscles. The weightlifter's arm muscles have grown thicker and stronger because he uses them often.
34	Pulse Points: Wrists, inside of ankles, inside of thighs, armpits, sides of head, right and left side of neck.
125	Green pepper, pea pod, cucumber, stringbean, corn, eggplant, avocado, zucchini.
178	1. Chocolate pudding 2. Cola soda 3. Instant chicken noodle soup 4. Dog food 5. Pop-Rocks

Dog food is the most nutritious of these five foods.

Glossary

AEROBIC

abdomen: the body cavity that contains the stomach and intestines.

abdominal: having to do with the abdomen.

adrenalin: a body chemical that speeds up the heartbeat and other body processes.

aerobic: using oxygen to release energy within the body.

allergy: a condition in which the body reacts to a foreign substance.

alveolus: one of the air sacs that make up the lungs (plural: **alveoli**).

amino acid: the chemical building block that is linked together in chains to form proteins.

anaerobic: not using oxygen to release body energy.

annual: a plant that completes its growth in one year.

antibody: a protein in the blood which helps the body fight off infection.

archaeologist: a person who studies earlier cultures by digging up and describing the materials they left behind.

artery: a tube-like vessel that carries blood from the heart to the other parts of the body.

bacterium: a one-celled organism that usually lives in or on plants or animals (plural: **bacteria**).

biennial: a plant that requires two years to complete its growth.

body composition: the amounts of fat and non-fat tissues that make up an individual's body weight.

breath volume: the amount of air a person takes in with each breath.

breathing rate: the number of breaths a person takes in a minute.

bronchial tube: one of the branches of the trachea (windpipe) that carry air into the lungs.

bronchitis: a disease that affects the bronchial tubes and prevents the lungs from getting rid of dirt and mucus.

calcium: a mineral that helps build bones and teeth.

calorie: a measure of the amount of energy stored in a food.

capillary: one of the tiny blood vessels where the exchange of oxygen, food, and waste takes place between the blood and the rest of the body tissues.

carbohydrate: a substance in food (such as starch or sugar) that provides fuel for the body.

carbon dioxide: an invisible, odorless gas that is produced when muscles burn food for energy, and is released from the body by exhaling.

carbon monoxide: a poisonous, invisible gas that is produced when tobacco burns.

cardio-respiratory: having to do with the heart and lungs.

cardio-respiratory endurance: the part of fitness that comes from a strong heart and healthy lungs.

cartilage: strong, flexible tissue that connects the surfaces of the bones.

cartilage disc: a round, flat piece of cartilage that connects two vertebrae in the backbone.

cell: a small structure, usually seen only under a microscope, which is the basic unit of the human body and of all other animals and plants.

cilium: one of the millions of tiny hairs in the windpipe and bronchial tubes that sweep out mucus and dirt (plural: **cilia**).

circulatory system: the network of arteries, veins, and capillaries through which the blood flows as it travels through the body.

complete protein: a food containing all the eight amino acids that the body cannot make for itself.

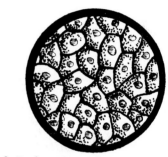

SKIN CELLS

BLOOD CELLS

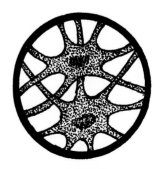

NERVE CELLS

DEHYDRATE

constipation: a condition in which the feces remain in the large intestine too long, lose too much moisture, and become hard and dry and difficult to move.

contract: to become smaller by drawing together, tightening.

coronary: having to do with the heart muscle.

coronary artery: one of the blood vessels that supplies oxygen to the heart.

cross-pollination: the process by which pollen is carried by wind or insects from flower to flower.

dehydrate: to dry out, remove all water from.

diarrhea: a condition in which the feces are moved too quickly out of the large intestine, and are watery.

emphysema: a disease caused by the breakdown of air sacs in the lungs.

environment: the surroundings that affect the life and growth of a living being.

enzyme: a chemical substance produced within body cells that helps to speed up the body's processes.

ethnic: sharing similar language, customs, and background.

ETHNIC

evaporation: the process by which water is lost to the surrounding air.

fat: a food substance that provides energy to the body.

fat cell: a cell that stores body fat.

fiber: the part of a plant food which cannot be digested and helps to move wastes out of the body.

fight-or-flight response: the combination of body changes that occurs in animals when they are excited or in danger.

flatus: gas that is made by bacteria in the large intestine.

flexibility: the ability to move easily in different directions.

fluoride: a mineral that helps strengthen teeth against decay.

gluten: a sticky protein present in flours, which helps bread to rise.

heartburn: a feeling of pain around the heart, caused by acid backing up from the stomach to the esophagus.

hemoglobin: the protein in red blood cells that contains iron and oxygen.

hydrogenation: adding hydrogen to vegetable oils to make them more solid.

incomplete protein: a food that is missing or is low in one or more of the eight essential amino acids.

iron: a mineral that helps carry oxygen through the bloodstream to all parts of the body.

joint: the place where two bones join together.

knead: to work with dough until it is smooth and elastic.

lung capacity: the total amount of space in the lungs.

malnutrition: a condition that results from too little food or a poorly balanced diet.

maximum heart rate: the fastest rate at which a person's heart can beat, depending on age, size, and how fit he/she may be.

meditation: a process that clears the mind and thoroughly relaxes the body.

EVAPORATION

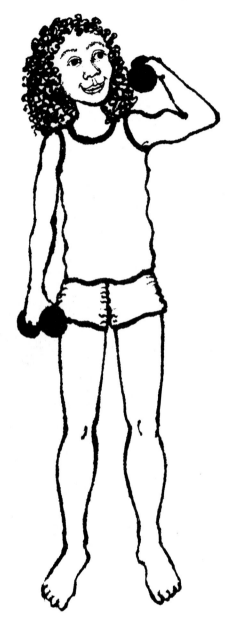

MUSCLE TONE

mineral: a nutrient which is part of the body's composition and is necessary for health and growth.

muscle: a body organ that can contract and relax to make other body parts move.

muscle endurance: the ability of a group of muscles to continue to work over a long period of time.

muscle fiber: a long, thin cell that joins with many others to make up a muscle.

muscle power: the ability to use muscle strength very quickly.

muscle strength: the greatest amount of work a group of muscles can do in a single effort.

muscle tone: firmness in a muscle or group of muscles.

nicotine: a poison that is the main active ingredient of tobacco.

nutrient: a substance needed by the body to grow and repair itself.

nutrition: the science that studies the nutrients in foods and how the body handles them.

obesity: an accumulation of excess fat in the body.

overload principle: strengthening a muscle or group of muscles by gradually increasing how often, how long, and how hard you exercise them.

overweight: weighing more than 10% above the ideal weight for one's height and bone structure.

oxygen: an invisible, odorless gas, without which muscles cannot burn food for energy.

perennial: a plant that lives for several years.

physically fit: able to lead an active life.

pollinate: to transfer pollen from the male part of a flower (the anther) to the female part (the stigma), usually by wind or insects.

polyunsaturated fat: vegetable oil, usually liquid at room temperature.

processing: changing food from its natural state.

protein: a substance in foods that is used for the body to grow and repair itself.

protein deficiency: a lack of enough complete proteins in the diet, often resulting in illness and poor growth.

pulse: the regular beat of the arteries caused by the flow of blood into the arteries from the pumping heart.

pulse rate: the number of times a person's pulse beats in one minute (equal to his/her heart rate).

pulse recovery: the return of the pulse to its resting rate after exercise.

red blood cell: one kind of cell that makes up the blood and carries oxygen to the other cells in the body.

refined sugar: sugar which has been purified and crushed into small grains.

relax: to become looser, less tense.

relaxation response: the slowing down of body processes through meditation.

REFINED SUGAR

saturated fat: fat that is usually solid at room temperature, generally from animals or animal products.

self-image: the idea or picture in a person's mind of how he/she looks and acts.

species: a group of plants or animals that share the same characteristics and may interbreed with one another.

staple: a food that is the main source of nutrients for people in a particular country or part of a country.

stigma: the sticky part of a flower which receives the grains of pollen.

STRESS

stress: changes in people's lives or feelings that make them feel excited or upset.

taproot: the large main root of a plant, out of which smaller roots may grow.

target zone: a heart or pulse rate that equals about 3/4 of a person's maximum heart or pulse rate.

tendon: a strong cord of tissue that connects a muscle to a bone.

tranquilizer: a drug used to slow down body processes and reduce stress.

ulcer: a small hole that stomach acid burns in the linings of some people's stomachs.

vegetarian: a person who eats no meat, choosing to eat only plant foods or a combination of plant foods, milk products, and eggs.

vein: a tube-like vessel that carries blood from all parts of the body towards the heart.

vertebra: one of the small bones that make up the backbone (plural: **vertebrae**).

vitamin: a nutrient necessary in tiny amounts for all body functions.

vomiting: throwing up partially digested food back from the stomach and out of the mouth.

yoga: a system of exercises from ancient India that gently stretch and relax all parts of the body.

YOGA